# Contemporary Indian Dramatists

# Contemporary Indian Dramatists

*Editor*
Shubha Tiwari

ATLANTIC
PUBLISHERS & DISTRIBUTORS (P) LTD

Published by

**ATLANTIC**

**PUBLISHERS & DISTRIBUTORS (P) LTD**

7/22, Ansari Road, Darya Ganj,
New Delhi-110002
Phones : +91-11-40775252, 23273880, 23275880, 23280451
Fax : +91-11-23285873
Web : www.atlanticbooks.com
E-mail : orders@atlanticbooks.com

Branch Office
5, Nallathambi Street, Wallajah Road,
Chennai-600002
Phones : +91-44-64611085, 32413319
E-mail : chennai@atlanticbooks.com



Printed in India at Glorious Printers, A-13, D.S.I.D.C., Jhilmil Industrial Area, Delhi-110095

# Editorial

Twentieth century has been the century of the novel. Fiction somehow suits the modern man. It not only expresses the complexities of modern life accurately; its mode of receiving (sitting or lying at home and reading) also suits the modern man. One can relax with a novel just anywhere and be lost in the fictional world. It is a readily available means to escape from the urgent affairs at hand. Drama, on the other hand, requires effort. It demands participation. Dramas are written to be staged and watched and not just read. This is a basic constraint in our understanding of drama. Watching a Shakespearean tragedy is an entirely different experience from reading it.

In the current scenario of information bombardment, cinema-invasion, television hijack, monopoly of the novel and apathy of the viewers, certain stalwarts have kept Indian dramatic scene alive. Theatre has been kept alive at chosen art-conscious centers like Mumbai, Kolkata, Bangalore and Delhi. For the rest of India, it is troops visiting once in a while and the audience gathering to watch 'the odd thing' out. State sponsored drama festivals have also helped in keeping this art form alive. Nevertheless, we may reiterate that governments cannot keep any art alive, particularly drama, which necessarily is a criticism of contemporary times. You cannot criticize your sponsor. And there ends the art and begins the art of flattery. It is public participation alone which can ultimately keep this art form alive. Audience, as we all know, is the real actor, the actual protagonist of any play.

There is no alternative to dramatic art. Direct viewing and the catharsis are too bold an experience to be compared to anything else. Even today, the craftiest womanizer cannot watch scenes of sinful liaisons being directly played. He will simply run away. The scoundrel wants to avoid Falstaff at any cost and the miser cannot watch a Shylock. The power of the drama cannot be questioned. You just have to watch a play to experience it. Cinema cannot match it; it is only a poor substitute to it. Drama is real. It is actual. It is the 'happening' thing. It is the 'do' thing rather than merely the 'watch' thing. You cannot be a bystander when it comes to drama. Either you are involved or you are out. There is no middle path.

In the first three papers, I have tried to understand and explain certain basic Indian and Western concepts of aesthetics, poetics and dramatalogy. Bharata's viewpoint on drama is extremely rational as well as practical. Studying Indian aesthetic concepts in comparison to the Western ones gives totality to our understanding of drama. Concepts like catharsis have earlier found expression in Indian thought but in different words.

In the present book we have tried to present some dimensions of contemporary dramatic scene in the country. My paper on Vijay Tendulkar's *Silence! The Court is in Session* has taken into consideration the social message imbibed in the play. Even as I was writing the play from Ms Benare's point of view, counter-views kept on cropping up somewhere in the other corners of my mind. It is true that female sexuality is a thing of guilt in this great land of 'rishis' and 'munis', nevertheless canalization of instincts is also not a very bad idea. We should relook at the path Benare took. However, the judgment, the hypocrisy of the judges, the meanness born out of double standards—all these are valid themes raised by this play. In the next paper, Dipika Sahai again takes up social message conveyed through the plays of Nissim Ezekiel. Ezekiel's plays are more urban and sophisticated in approach than Tendulkar's. Needless to add, however, that Ezekiel's reputation rests on his poems rather than his plays. Then comes a paper by Ashok Kumar Sharma who has analyzed *Ghasiram Kotwal* from different angles. *Ghasiram Kotwal* is a gory play. It is very raw and generates such responses. Crime, murder, womanizing, conspiracy—these cannot be called by soft names. In the next paper, again on *Ghasiram Kotwal*, Smita Mishra has discussed it as a political play. Crimes that violate our sensibilities are everyday phenomena in politics. Murder, treachery, womanizing—all these are common features of politics. There never was any politics without the famous three Ws. The parameters are patriarchal. Women are mere things, gifts to exchange in this dirty game. Then comes a paper by Jayadeep Sarangi that compares and contrasts two plays of Girish Karnad—*Hayavadana* and *Tughlaq*. It is interesting to see how Karnad has woven a fabric out of myth, history and traditions in these two plays. Different symbols taken from different sources mingle and form a beautiful pattern. Prayer is an important symbol in *Tughlaq*. In my opinion, it is the key symbol of the play. When prayer is polluted, the very source of life gets filthy. Nothing can purify a mind whose prayers have gone dirty. Prayer is an end in itself; prayer for an end is no prayer at all. Prayer is unconditional submission to Almighty. The discussion on myths is carried on further in the next paper by Ranjana Chanana who has taken up *The Fire and The Rain*. The paper is inspired by Indian poetics and rightly so. In the next paper, Sadhana Agrawal has taken up theology and monarchy in *Tughlaq*. Then, Kranti Mishra has discussed symbolism in *Tughlaq* while Roopesh Chaturvedi and Rohini Dubey has commented on Karnad as a dramatist. Smita Mishra, in her article, has given a general estimation of Tendulkar as a playwright.

The papers in the present book are more or less based on relation of contemporary drama to real life problems and situations. It is earnestly hoped that the collection will prove useful and interesting to concerned scholars.

**Shubha Tiwari**

# Contents

# Bharata's Viewpoint on Drama

1

*Shubha Tiwari*

"Whenever and wherever the humans have progressed beyond the mere struggle for existence, gods, recreation and self-expression, there has been a theatre in some sense." Drama constitutes a very important part of literature and Indian literature is one of the oldest literatures of the world. Since ages Sanskrit drama has remained the most beautiful and vital part of Indian literature. It is well-known that the expression of sentiments and feelings of man through gestures and speech laid the seeds of drama, which is a reflection of life, of the emotions of the three worlds. Sage Bharata defines drama as an imitation of action in these words:

> "The drama is an imitation of the emotions (bhava) of the three worlds."
>
> "The drama has been devised by me as an imitation of actions and conducts of people."
>
> "An imitation of the world with its seven division has been made the basis of drama."

The dramatists present events that generate emotions around them and the readers in turn receive aesthetic pleasure. Our Indian classical dramatists hold this view. Tradition of drama in India is glorious and pristine. The *Natyasastra* is the most voluminous and comprehensive study on dramaturgy. Bharatmuni is the author of the *Natyasastra*, which has remained since long the only text on dramaturgy. The *Natyasastra* encompasses within itself elements not only of drama but also of music and dance. The title *Natyasastra* literally means "the science of drama" and Bharata has taken into account theatre organization, along with various aspects of drama. The treatise is generally believed to have been composed between 200 B.C. and 200 A.D.

The origins of the drama have always been rooted in the religious instincts of mankind. The origins of Sanskrit drama is the most interesting aspect and scholars have held different views of its origin. The traditional account given in the *Natyasastra* according to which Brahma created the fifth Veda at a time people came under the influence of lust and greed and wasted their time and money in the pursuit of materialistic gains. Indra along with other gods approached Brahma and requested him to create an object of diversion. Thus, he created drama by taking recitation from the Rigveda, song from the Samveda, and aesthetics from the Atharvaveda. Bharatamuni was then assigned the task to bring this fifth Veda to the earth.

Apart from the account given in the *Natyasastra*, scholars have calculated the dramatic form to have inculcated from the singing of Vedic hymns, shadow plays and mimes, and dance. Dance is a part and parcel of drama; it has obviously supported drama with its various rhythmic movements. Whatever be the origin of drama, the minute details present in the *Natyasastra* are evident of the long tradition of Sanskrit drama.

Bharatamuni's *Natyasastra* is much wider in range and scope than Aristotle's *Poetics*. *Natyasastra* is a comprehensive book that discusses all aspects of dramaturgy. Natyasastra has been under study by scholars and they have elaborated its contents from time to time. Bharata deals with the nature of drama in the very first chapter of the *Natyasastra*. He laid down various tenets for dramatists, as well as, actors and directors, as they are important constituents of drama. The task of a dramatist is the most difficult one, since he has to present a piece of work, which is audible as well as visible. The function of drama is not merely entertainment but it also serves the purpose of instruction. Unlike the Western tradition, drama aims at the depiction and presentation of emotions to the audience. The purpose of Sanskrit drama is the preservation of moral values of the society, and thereby raising them through dramatic activity.

The first step towards dramatization of events is the choice of a theme. Here lies the important task of a dramatist. "If *rasa* is the soul of drama, *plot* is the body of drama", says Bharata. A dramatist fixes an object of achievement and the achiever, designs a plot or theme for the purpose. Bharata states that the plot is of two kinds: the principal (*adhikarika*) and subsidiary (*prasangika*). The principal plot involves the action of the hero for attainment of position or material advantage. The subsidiary plot comprises of actions, which indirectly lead to make the theme a composite one. The dramatist has to divide the plot into acts. The acts should be independent, and at the same time should appear as a whole so as to impart unity. The five elements of the plot are the germ (*bija*), the prominent point (*bindu*), the episode (*pataka*), the episodical incident (*prakari*) and the enactment (*karya*).

Bharata speaks of five explanatory devices (*artho pakse paka*), which means communication of incidents and facilitate the dramatist to convey the facts or actions which need much time or space. This way he also imparts compactness to the play. These explanatory devices are: The explanatory scene (*viskambha*), the intimating scene (*pravesaka*), the continuing scene (*ankavatara*) and the anticipatory scene (*ankamukha*). Further he describes the five stages of action, which lead to the fulfillment of the objective. The stages of action and the elements of plot are linked by junctures (*sandhis*), five in number. They denote the composition of each stage of action in the play. Not only this, Bharata has assigned specific time for the period of a particular play. The scene of the plot must be laid in the cultural soil. The unities of time, place and action should be maintained. The events or actions connected with a particular stage should be mentioned within an act, so that the scene of action may not be so far that the hero may not reach within a specified time period.

Bharata describes about the characters in the Chapter XXXIV of the *Natyasastra* and explains the types of characters an their qualities in detail. He also elaborates the qualities and types of hero and other characters as well.

The *Natyasastra* ascribes ten kinds of plays. The term *rupaka* is used instead of some action or events, emotions and feelings, in which a person is confronted to some situation which in turn brings *pleasure* or *pain*. Thus it brings delight to the eyes too, and hence the term *rupaka* is used. The ten varieties of *rupaka* are as: *nataka, prakarna, bhana, prahasana, dima, vyayoga, samavakara, vithi* and *anka*.

According to Indian traditional dramatic theories a play should present a basic mental state and it should occupy a central position in the play.

> "There is nothing—no knowledge, no skill, no science, no art, no yoga, no activity—that is not seen in drama."

Poetry is the highest form of art and drama is the highest form of poetry. They are complementary to each other. Drama is the product of a civilized and cultural society. Drama in India originated out of the need for entertainment. The gods approached Brahma to create an object of diversion, (*Kridaniyka*) as the people of that time were addicted to sensual pleasures and were under the spell of desire and greed and thus brought upon misery and sorrow. So Brahma created the *Natyaveda* or fifth Veda, which would serve not only the function of entertainment but also of instruction. Thus, the drama as Bharata mentions is an artifice just like a toy. Its sole purpose is to provide amusement and instruction to the people.

Thus, Bharata gives equal weightage to instruction, as well as, to entertainment. The Indian concept of drama has rather been serious as compared to the Western concept. Indian concept of drama is the production of an emotional delight, a pure and elevated pleasure. Bharata believes that drama instructs through entertainment and entertains through instruction. When a playwright desires to give some instructions, he does not simply give away emotions but represents them through action and injects them into the heart and mind of his audience.

The process of dramatic art is like that of a tree—The germ, the sprout, the development of the tree into branches, flowers and fruits. The seed attains fulfillment on giving fruits. In a similar manner drama attains fulfillment on the arousal of *rasa* or dramatic experience. Bharata observes, "The theme or plot is the bulk of natya." The germ or the plot forms the basis, the framework on which drama is constructed. Whether it is read or seen, the dramatist cannot execute his art without undergoing the process of plot construction.

The plot or theme of the play is actually the message the playwright wants to convey. The play has a major and related themes. The plot is framework of a drama wherein the series of incidents are interrelated to make up the story for drama. All the incidents and characters are so related as to lead the plot to a climax, which is artistically satisfying.

The subject matter of drama is usually the life of a person, whether historical, contemporary or imaginary. The Western dramatist aims at the presentation of a character manifesting itself in action. On the other hand, the Indian dramatist aims at the presentation of a basic mental state at a place where it is relishable. Our stress is on *rasa*, theirs on catharsis. Thus in the presentation of drama, action occupies central place in the Western concept and the basic mental state occupies central position in the Indian concept. In both the situations, it is characters that occupy a prominent place; whether it is depiction of action or of emotion.

The object of Sanskrit dramatist is different and so his choice of the material also has to be different. The presentation is meant for an audience who seeks aesthetic pleasure. A dramatist is expected to maintain harmony and unity in his production. Whatever he presents on the stage and all that he makes the characters speak, must perfectly harmonize with the basic mental state, which is primarily to be presented. Once the dramatist has analyzed the plot, the hero has to be fixed. The main story represents the hero in pursuit of achieving his goal. In the course of the development of plot, when the dramatist wants to present a particular mental stage and particular traits he pays attention to the hero. The hero or protagonist is set with some events and situations and his personality is thus highlighted. The protagonist acquires an important position as it is through him the various emotions are presented. The protagonist is the chief character in the play through whom the emotions and gist of the play are depicted. The events of the play move around the central character or the protagonist.

Drama presents fiction or fact in a scene that can be acted before an audience. A play has a plot, characters, dialogue and an outlook on life, it is not only read but it is written with a purpose to be staged. Unlike other forms of art, drama is such an art in which the author, the actors and the stage manager all contribute towards producing the dramatic effect. Drama like other arts is a representation of life. A great play is the product of imagination, working upon experience and observation.

Character is the very soul of drama as it is the character through whom the dramatist can bring out different issues into focus. A character is that person in a play with a brief descriptive sketch who identifies particular traits and qualities. These qualities which a character typifies, are experienced through dialogues and what they do is the action. The portrayal of the character, his actions, manner of thought, personality, his qualities and traits are what is termed as characterization. This involves care and ability on the part of the dramatist to create and depict a character so that it is perceived well by the readers and viewers.

In Aristotle's *Poetics* as well as in Bharata's *Natyasastra*, characterization is discussed in detail. Aristotle lays down four qualities that are essential for the characters of a tragedy. Bharata had devoted the whole chapter No. XXXIV to the explanation of the various types of characters and their qualities. Bharata deals with characters and says that characters either male or female generally are of three types—superior (*uttama*), middling (*madhyama*) and inferior (*adhama*). Characterization and plot have a strong correlation with each other.

Literature simply implies written words, which are valuable in terms of beauty of language and emotional effect. Literature provides a memorable effect. Literature provides a memorable experience and it provokes the imaginative sense of the reader. It is true that life is not literature and literature is not life. Readers perceive and understand the importance of literature when the reality of life and the imagination of literature are brought together. A reader's experience with a book is the same as his experience with the other objects of life. In literature as well as in life, the magic of imagination creates vivid images that may develop in the reader a disposition to accept the images as physical reality. It is important that there should be a correspondence between real experience provided by nature and virtual experience provided by literature.

A work of literary art has within itself a unity, a completed pattern of wholeness which is in itself one of the sources of the particular pleasure given by literature. When a piece of literature is presented on stage the readers falls easy victim to the illusion of reality, the characters are living and breathing, the settings are real. A moment's reflection will dispel the illusion as effectively as the reflection that the novel is only a story or that the poem is just something made by the poet.

Drama is the product of an essentially cultured condition of a nation. The exact point of the evolution of the theatre is hidden deep in diverse forms and confused accounts. Whether it is divine or human, religious or social, spiritual or secular, it is organically related to the human impulses which give rise to all our movements and gestures.

The origin of the drama is closely connected with the religious trinity (1) Brahma (2) Vishnu and (3) Mahesvara.

Bharata in the very beginning of his *Natyasastra*, pays obeisance to Brahma and Mahesvara for no other reason than that be the originator of drama and later to be the originator of dance. Furthermore Brahma, is supposed to have borrowed its various aspects from different Vedas and their subsidiary branches. Thus, he is said to have borrowed the art of effective speech or elocution from the Yajur Veda and the *rasas* from the Atharva Veda.

"na hi rasad rte kascid arthah pravartate, tatre vibhavanubhave vyabhicarisamyogad rasanispattih."

This means "no object can be comprehended without the aid of *Rasa*. Sentiment is produced from a combination of determinants, consequents the transitory states. In other words, when the dominant or permanent states come in contact with transitory feelings, they result in the awakening of *rasa*, a complete state of enjoying the flavour."

*Rasa* literally means juice, essence or flavour. Whether the relish implies to that of Aryan's drinking of the som juice, or the yogi's communication with the comic soul or the reader's delightful experience of a beautiful piece of literature.

*Rasa* as meaningful word had floated in the air of ancient India for a very ling time. It figures in Rig Veda, and in the Upanishads. The first work in which *rasa* has been used in an aesthetic content and with an aesthetic purpose is the *Natyasastra*. For Bharata, it meant a distinct school of thought. One of the most important qualities of any literature or any work art is that it attracts attention. But this is not enough in Indian tradition, not only should the work draw attention but it must also appeal. The *rasa* occurs in the sixth chapter of the *Natyasastra*. He says in the chapter:

"Vibhavanubhava-vyabhicari-samyogad rasanispattih".

It means that the realization of *rasa* results from the union of *vibhava*, *anubhava* and *vyabhichari bhava*.

Just as flavour comes from a combination of many spices, herbs and other substances, so *rasa* from many *bhavas*. *Rasa* is more than an amalgam of taste and smell. It is as self revelation, a realization of truth, a coming closer to the living light. *Rasa* is superb bliss (*ananda*), for the soul aspires for bliss. Vedic view is that man in his spiritual nature and in his truest being is *rasa* himself. *Rasa* involves total identification. It is a state when the personality or ego does not intrude. Total identification implies loss of personal identity.

The *Natyasastra* lists eight *rasas*, but scholars believe that the ninth *rasa* i.e., *santa rasa* is of later addition. These *rasas* have strong emotional content. *Natyasastra* strongly emphasizes the fact that the object of art is pleasure. And art must come through a medium that is pleasurable: also it must not hurt anyone. These features of providing pleasure or delight bring all the categories of *rasas* under one category. Thus all *rasas* are pleasurable though the emotional content behind this pleasure is different.

Bharata's conception of *rasa* is that *rasa* is an object, which is responsible for aesthetic experience. Not only this his cancers also involved in showing the necessary constituents of *rasa* and their muted relation, and with the means and methods of its presentation.

The *Natyasastra* aims at *rasopattih*, the evocation of *rasa*. Sanskrit drama pays sincere attention to plot, character, language and diction of dramatic representation. The characters of hero-heroine, all placed in well-defined categories, provide the best scope for the delineation of the precise *rasa* that is to achieve full force and felicity.

Drama makes use of visible as well as audible characters. When it is enacted, the play makes full use of all aspects for dramatic effect. Language along with gestures becomes a valuable tool for the expression of meaning.

Moreover, the first appeal of art is to the sense, and through senses, art aims to awaken an emotional state. Drama is a complete form of art meant both for the ear and eye, graphic and auditory mediums. It is a miniature representation of the world of human affectations, the noble and exemplary aspects of society. The aim is recreation of life. Drama serves to moralize through its powers of reorientation of the mind. This dramatic effect is created by the dramatist through *rasa anubhuti*.

Aristotle says that "drama is an imitation of action", but Bharata, never regards drama as a crude imitation. Aristotle interpreted that by 'men in action' means thing happening in terms of human nature, events that are embodied in human lives, but Bharata has explained his views regarding drama "that a drama gives an account of acts and ideas." Imagination according to Bharata, is essential to drama. He says, "in it there is no exclusive representation of you or of the gods; for the drama is a representation of an action of Avastha." "The drama devised by me is a mimicry of action and conduct of people, which is rich in various emotions and which depicts different situations. This will relate to actions of men—good, bad and indifferent, and will give courage, amusement and happiness as well as counsel to them all." All this is an imitation of action and the conduct of people, rich in various emotions in different situations. Aristotle says that poetry can imitate people as they are or people who could be better and worse than the average. Bharata and Aristotle mean more or less the same thing by imitation.

The Indian concept of drama has rather been serious as compared to the Western concept. The subject matter of drama is usually the life of a person whether historical, contemporary or imaginary. The Western dramatist aims at the presentation of a character manifesting itself in action. On the other hand, Indian dramatist aims at the presentation of a basic mental state at a place where it is relishable. Thus in the presentation of drama, action occupies a central place in the Western concept. In the Indian concept, the mental state is of prime concern.

## REFERENCES

Adolphus William Ward, *A History of English Literature*, Vol. I (India, 1997).

Cheney Sheldon, Int., *Theatre: 3000Yrs.*

Ifar Evans, *A Short History of English Literature* (Great Britain, 1966).

Janet Spens, *Elizabethan Drama* (London, 1922).

Janet Spens, *Elizabethan Drama* (London, 1992).

S.H. Butcher, *Aristotle's Poetry and Fine Art.*

Satish Kumar, *A History of English Literature.*

*The Natyasastra*, Chater – I, English translation by Manmohan Ghosh.

Thomas Mare Parrote, et al., *A Short View of Elizabethan Drama* (USA, 1943).

William Henry Hudson, *An Outline History of English Literature* (New Delhi, 2000).

# Western and Indian Concepts of Aesthetics

2

*Shubha Tiwari*

There is a lot of confusion about the beginning of Aesthetics. There was a time when Greece was regarded as the radiating centre of major world cultures, East and West. Then came the Diffusionist School of W.J. Perry and Eliot Smith that "all higher civilizations of the world came from ancient Egypt." Now with a deeper probe into the subject, the Dark continent has come to new light. What we call Egyptian is in essence an African inspiration. Asian influences percolated into it later.

Where do we begin in Aesthetics, from the West or India? The one answer is: begin from beginning, the pre-historical, the Paleolithic through Mesolithic and Neolithic eras; copper, bronze and iron ages, that is from the art of primitive civilizations.

## THE PRIMITIVE ART (PRIMITIVE IN HISTORICAL SENSE)

Even the modern art of Europe derives its inspiration from the highly abstract symbolic art of Africa: masks and bizarre animal and human figures. The primitive man shaping his flint weapons was behaving as an artist, that is as a man of skill and beauty, which idea is conveyed by the Greek word: techne. His simple mind had not broken up the living whole into the useful and the beautiful as we do today. Even the decorative motif was not separated.

Primitive art was, by and large, religious and symbolic. A mask, for example, had a meaning and purpose to drive away any evil to the wearer. A figurine like the 40,000 years old mother goddess, with big bosoms and buttocks, was regarded as the giver of all goods: fertility of the earth and woman, a rich harvest and children.

We once hailed primitive art as simple. But when we analysed it from the closer point of view, the art historians discovered that the primitive art techniques of abstractions and distortion of forms were highly purposeful and pragmatic, and not caused by any lack of skill. To those wedded to imitation theories, believing that the artistic creativity begins with being photographic, it came as a shock to know that the primitive masks and figures served the hieratic purpose as nothing else could, not the least a photocopy imitation. This purposeful distortion required a high order abstraction, i.e. separating some aspects from a reality that suits the religious objective. This moulding a thing to serve a specific purpose, called plastic skill, is the essence of art. This fact frees the primitive art from the sins of naturalism and naïve realism, which means to accept nature as it is without transmuting it.

We must skip over the vast treasures of the primitive art, scattered over the world so that we may concentrate on its aesthetic part only. It is art of great *meaning (symbolic)*, of great *significance (functional)*, of *power* and *energy (dynamic)* and of deep *spiritual exuberance* (having an inner dimension), and above all, *a proof positive of creative will.*

Its importance for aesthetics lies in that it evolved all the formal principles of beauty. Frank Willet observes: The criteria of beauty as symmetry about the vertical axis, coupled with balance, rhythm and harmony between the various masses, surfaces and lines, criteria which we tend to appreciate intuitively rather than measure it in an objective way, are all embedded in this art.

## EGYPTIAN CONTRIBUTION

From pre-historic Africa to pre-historic Egypt, transition is smooth: "The art of pre-dynamic Egypt shows essentially African characteristics, ...a rigidity of form, a frontality of pose, a lack of facial expression and an absence of any clear indication of age and subject, features which are characteristics of African statues."

The Egyptian statues are very similar to ancestor figures from many parts of Africa; they are repository of supernatural force; in particular, they provide a residence for all eternity for the spiritual essence of the man represented. "It was an attempt of art to eliminate all movements so that a statue could present and preserve a vision of immobility and immortality, of eternity and divinity. This is, as it were, man becoming god, to divinize the human! Such a statue was sculpted after "a magical ritual which ensured that it became imbued with the spirit of dead man."

This compares well with the Indian scriptures and the Chinese canonical literature laying down *dhyana mantras* and *magic formulae* with fasting and other purifactory practices. The aim, however, was not, to divinize man but to create a deity in a mere stone slab for worship.

## THE GREEK AESTHETICS

If the Egyptian art aimed at achieving immobility and immortality in what was human and temporal, thus conferring divinity on man through artistic device, the Greek art achieved its opposite by freeing the statue of its statism and investing it with vital energy and movement. Thus the Greek art proceeded to humanize Hellenic gods or to divinize their men. If man is the model of perfection, of beauty and grace, man must be the Greek Hero." Then man becomes the measure of all things. From this cardinal notion follows the formula of Greek Aesthetics: Mimesis, Imitation or Representation in Art. Art imitates or represents reality.

Several other points follow from the mimetic theory of art:

(a) If art imitates, it imitates what? What is the nature of reality itself? Plato was an Idealist, a philosopher to whom there is a universe of Ideas, of Absolute, or of Archetypes of which our mundane world is a shadow, never reaching the supermundane universe of the Absolute. Art is therefore, illusion; full of charm, therefore bad for young folk.

(b) Aristotle accepted the mimetic idom of artistic creation, but rejected the photographic imitation of reality. No art can create a horse on a piece of paper, or in a block of stone. But an artist can represent concept of horseness; a type of idea about the concept which he has in his mind, i.e., a notion of horse that can be found nowhere except in the rational mind of man. It means not a horse as it is, but as it can and should be, not a horse but an idea of horse, horseness itself. Art universalizes an object. It need not idealise it.

(c) As to art experience, Plato thought it is a deception caused by the illusory nature of art. To Aristotle, artistic experience purges the mind of its emotional loadings like hatred, cruelty, horror etc. This purge of the mind is always observed in Greek Tragedy. This is Aristotle's principle of Catharsis.

(d) Rational, Ethical and Artistic elements characterize the Hellenic culture. Its ethics, the sense of the good, is derived from its art, the sense of the beautiful, which means balance and harmony, proportion and rhythm. These are the formal principles of beauty. So form is the essence of artistic creation.

(e) The form is for contemplation, a rational activity of the mind, or, as Socrates would say, "the activities of the soul", and not for emotionalization. Emotions are not only to the purged from the mind. Rational contemplation of form is joy-giving as mathematics did to *Pythagoras*.

After the mind has been cleansed, the tragic experience of beauty in a drama gives light and joy to the contemplative mind.

(f) Art continues to be religious in Greek as in Egypt. The Greek tragedies were not staged for public entertainment. "Religious approach of Greek tragedies was meant for profound contemplation of eternal truths." Tragedy reveals these truths, and it results from "the encounter of man with more than man." (Sophocles)

(g) The Greek art is realistic. Tragedy was a reality of Greek life *exposed* to all manner of horrors of the Heroic age: wars were common and a way of life.

(h) The greatest contribution of Greek art is its free creation. Gina Pishel sums it up as follows: "The focal points of Greek art are its lucidity and rationality, its art form founded on intelligence more than on power, realization of the intrinsic values of form and expression of *the values* of balance, harmony, order, proportion and moderation. It was founded on clear, sound principles of rationality on man's desire to be aware of the outside world by imposing his laws upon it."

The supernatural form plays no part in Greek art, which sought to extol life's warmth and beauty, not the world beyond the grave so that the *noble* beauty of the human form became the most convincing image of the idea of the divine principle. In the name of superiority and serenity of reason, it imposed upon reality—its laws of order, balance and clarity.

## THE CHRISTIAN ART AND RENAISSANCE

Rome is extrovert and outgoing. Christianity gave to art, for the first time, or new experience to the West, an inwardness, introversion and a spiritual dimension, unknown even to the Greeks.

The Christian art spreads over to many centuries and countries, made great and rich contribution to a new experience of beauty: simplicity, spiritual inwardness, symbolism, allusiveness and humanism because of its stress on compassion and on embodiment of man's religious beliefs. There was a touch of transcendentalism also, looking beyond the physical barriers of existence towards heaven.

The Renaissance art of Italy is the high tide mark of artistic creativity both in quality and expanse. It is spread over three centuries and in many countries of Europe. But our concern is not its expanse or the background of cultural history of Europe. It is the aesthetic values of Renaissance art, which broke from the airiness and transcendentalism of Gothic art, and came close to the spirit of the Western Ethos and its European personality.

## INDIAN AESTHETICS

Max Muller and many others including him, doubted the possibility of Indian Aesthetics, since, according to them, there is no equivalent of the term "beautiful" in Sanskrit, and our paintings, sculptures and creative literature considered as works of art are "simply worthless." A.K. Coomarswamy speaks of oriental aesthetic theory, where 'oriental to him means mainly Indian. If as we believe, man is an aesthetic being, creating and fashioning, expressing and impressing, imposing his mind on matter and his purpose on a material medium, it is strange if Indians were devoid of any sense of beauty and form, and without any art and aesthetics!

On the contrary, India has given to the world a metaphysics of beauty in terms of *rupa* and *rasa* and a fully developed psychoaesthetics in Bharata. There is perfect unity from the pre-Vedic through Vedic to post-Vedic ages of art traditions and art treasures as well as aesthetics and speculation.

The fact of history regarding Indian art is that it (Indian art) was born before its philosophy or spirituality. Indian art has its root in the soil of India. The fact of history is "that art was pursed with a conscious effort and permeated all aspects of life, enhancing its beauty.

## METAPHYSICS OF BEAUTY: THE CONCEPT OF 'RUPAM'

*Rupa* is translated as form, and by a form is implied a dualism of form and content which in India is never accepted.

In pre-Vedic India, the Neolithic art and the art of Indus civilization, a form is a form of life; its vigour and vitality, its joy and conquest of mere materiality.

Even Mario admits: "No wonder that from the very start Indian artists strove to render the secret streams of life flowing not only in men but in every living thing", and further: 'Sumerian art continued to express the supreme value through immobility'. But in India, "based on the flow and essence of life, the greatest stress was laid on rendering the movements of bodies at once the manifestation and rhythm of life."

There is an aesthetic value of immobility. It may yield a geometrical form and the formal principles of beauty. There is also an aesthetic value of movement, leading us to a vital form and the principles of rhythm and internal harmony. This vital form is *rupa* of Indian Aesthetics. It is the manifest (*vyakta*) order of the unmanifest (*avyakta*). The unmanifest is the surge of life, its manifestation is *rupa* in art. The two, however, are not separate with each other. Dance is the form of expressing rhythm of life, and its vital movement. So, in India, from the very beginning, dance becomes the art form, right from Shiva figures of Indus Valley to Natraja. Dance as manifesting "the flow and essence of life" becomes the core of Indian art, the basic idiom of all artistic creation.

## THE VEDIC CONCEPT OF 'RUPA'

Each form is a form of the formless, the Self, man's spiritual essence. It is the visible index of the invisible, the finite and sensuous experience of the infinite and supra-sensuous. Each form (*rupa*) is the manifest surrogate (*prati-rupa*) of the unmanifest:

> *Rupam-rupam prati rupan samhhabhuva....* From the pre-Vedic to the Vedic, we pass from the vital to the spiritual, without any change in the idiom of expression. Declare the Vedas: Kavi, ... the creator, creates all form. All forms are the forms of the self, which is *ananda* (joy), the essence of our being (*sat*... lying beyond the physical realm,—the realm of body, vital self form (*prana*), emotionality and intellect. The physical form is the form of the meta-physical, and in being so, the physical form is beautiful. This is in substance the Vedic metaphysics of beauty.

From the history of Indian civilization we came to know that we could not stay long at the spiritualistic metaphysics of the Vedas and the Upanishads. The *folk religions asserted themselves* over the elite Vedic culture, and art had to move from spirituality to divinity, from the transcendental self to the gods of common belief. So, a new definition of form to suit the folk spirit had to come: Each form is a form of the divinity.

This post-Vedic development of Indian art explains the entire pantheon of gods and goddesses.

Here the pre-Vedic elements are absorbed and assimilated with the post-Vedic. *Yakshas* are given a place in art, and their King *Kuber* a god in his own right. *Yakshini* becomes *Lakshmi*, the consort of Vishnu. Others are transfigured into *Jyotirlings*, the indexes of light divine. This was the greatest effort a culture could make for assimilation of any form of life.

A form is generally conceived as mathematical and geometric. Principles of form can be derived from it, and it is rationally contemplated. *Rupa* is metaphysical (meta-beyond) and always asks the viewer to go beyond (transcend) the barriers the physical—to the vital surge of life (pre-Vedic), to the spiritual self (Vedic), or to the divine (the post-Vedic and popular). This going beyond (transcendence) from the physical to the meta-physical is the essential quality of *rupa*.

If the mind sticks to the physical, the self, the immediate and the sensuous, and is not moved to go beyond, then no art has been created, no art has been enjoyed. Movement, both centripetal and centrifugal, from and to the work of art and beyond to the self, causes pleasant tensions in the mind-body systems, we simply call it *rasa*.

We stress this point because in the Western context, spirituality is a quality that does not belong to the material base. An artist spiritualizes as he creates qualities like softness, sweetness, lightness, tension and vigour, movement, balance etc. in a block of marble, which are not the qualities of the marble. These qualities are represented from reality, and enjoyed in the form of 'inner mimicry', resonance or mimesis. Indian art is anti-representation. It comes from within. It is not affected by rationalism or realism Transcendence, or going beyond is a dynamic quality of *rupa*.

## NATURE OF *RASA*: THE VEDIC VIEW

Vedic view is different from that of Bharata, though the term remains the same: *rasa*. The vedic view is that man in his spiritual nature and in his truest being is *rasa* himself. *Rasa* is joy (*ananda*) and light (*chit*) and life's innermost substance.... Which taking experience of an art form the onlooker (or, the listener) has to journey from the sensuous to the supra-sensuous by transcending the barriers caused by ego (*ahamkara*). These ego-barriers are the five *koshas* or sheaths (covering). The physical is the *annamaya kosha*, the body form, for e.g., the Tajmahal. There is nothing beyond what we see, beyond the body form lies the search of vitality. This is *pranamaya kosha*. Some art may stop here too, to give a vital and powerful 'feel of life'. Many divinities in stone, metal or wood, abound in the quality of dynamism, the *Varaha* figure or *Durga* or *Hanuman*. You feel life in their presence. Beyond it is the mental lane, *manomaya kosha*, where the mind itself is revealed in the matter. Emotions flow high and the mind is *stirred* up. The next is *Vizjnanamaya kosha*....), the plane of intellect—Great ideas may be embodied in art for intellectual realization. There are the ideas transfigured into images and the mind travels from the material to the imaginal plane. Beyond the intellect is 'you', your being and your truth, the self, the reality, transcending all ego-barriers. Its experience is *rasa*.

Now comes the Vedanta meta-psychology; to know is to be. To be is to be free from all false identifications of the self with the non-self. This identification is bondage (*bandhan*). Art experience frees man (*moksha*) from the inner bondage caused by ego. So long as the bondage is there, no true experience of joy is possible. In the moment of absorption (*laya*) the spectator is no more there standing apart from the grand spectacle. He is what he sees, listens to or experiences. His ego is transcended, and in a state of freedom he stands face to face with his truth and totality. *This experience is rasa.*

## BHARATA'S PSYCHO AESTHETICS

According to Vedic Aesthetics, the highest beauty experience is a *Samadhi*-like state. This is the state of our being as free, and transcending all ego-complexes. Art can lift the onlooker to self-realisation. Art belongs to the common man, the folk and experience of beauty cannot be divorced from the common human feelings. His will to form is His will to beauty. Art is therefore common man's property, the commonest of men, and not a privilege of any spiritual elite.

This brings us to Bharata's aesthetics, his psycho-aesthetics. Bharata need not have followed the Vedas, since the common man pre-existed the man of the Vedas. Bharata's is the common man's aesthetics, turning away from transcendentalism to psychology. Bharata, however remains true to the Vedas and true to the Indian traditional thought as well.

Bharata, the Doctor of *Rasa* emerges in a concrete shape, fully developed in all varied ramifications in *Natyashastra*. It deals with a variety of kindred art and science and among them are poetry, literary criticism, dramaturgy etc.

The theory of *Rasa* is an earnest attempt to indicate the character of emotional effect of drama. It successfully explains the rise and nature of aesthetic pleasure that a responsive audience experiences while witnessing the skilful enactment of a play. It was briefly stated by Bharata in his well known aphoristic style.

## REFERENCES

Gupteshwar Prasad, *I.A. Richards and Indian Theory of Rasa.*

H.L. Sharma, *Indian Aesthetic and Aesthetic Perspective.*

Priyadarshani Patnaik, *Rasa in Aesthetic.*

R.S. Singh, *The Poetics of I.A. Richards: A Collection of Critical Essays.*

# Vibhavanubhav Vyabhicharisyojat Rasnishpatti

3

*Shubha Tiwari*

Bharata formulates the grammar of Indian art:

1. Art is drama, and a drama is dramatization of feelings and actions on a stage and in a setting appropriate for communication with the spectator who has a heart (Sahridaya....).
2. Having a heart means that a spectator has an eye to see and ear for music, and above all, can respond to and reverberate in sympathy with what he sees and listens.
3. *Rasa* is that feeling, which is communicated to the spectator by the stage setting drama and all. *Rasa* is not a mere arousal of feeling or an emotional reaction to a situation. It is resonance, a psycho-neutral reverberation of body-mind system in response to drama.
4. To be is to be free and full of joy, was the Vedic Aesthetics. In Bharata, To be (*bhava*) is to feel as a human being, truly and fully. This feeling is communicated by the drama i.e., by dramatization and the stage setting (*vibhava*). To feel as a human being is abiding and inalienable nature to Bharata (*sthayibhava*). Art communicates to it with all the causative power (*vibhava*). This causation is the psycho-organic reverberation, within and without (*anubhava* and *samcharibhava*). The event thus, produced is *rasa* experience (*rasa nishpatti:* an uncommon experience, where being is feeling).
5. Bharata thus formulated a view of aesthetic causation along with his theory of aesthetic reality. Aesthetic reality-dance-form-beauty of rhythmic-expression, full

and free is drama and dramatization. The aesthetic causation is a form of communication. So, whatever fails to communicate is not beautiful.

## THE WORD *RASA*

What does the word *rasa* actually means? Any word itself, does not really mean anything. Its associations with time, context and other words only gives it a cloud of meanings. And the older a word becomes, the richer its associations, its resources, its cadence. So it is that a word can mean various things since its emergence.

*Rasa* at one time meant 'water', 'juice' or 'wine'. At another time it implied 'essence'. In another context it meant to 'relish' or 'savouring'. It also meant 'aesthetic pleasure' or 'enjoyment' – a meaning or association of meanings with which we are essentially concerned.

*Rasa* as a meaningful word has floated in the air of ancient Indian art for a very long time. It figures in Rig Veda, it figures in the Upanishads. It is also to be found in our ancient treatise on chemistry and medicine.

But the particular *rasa* with which we are concerned came much later and is to be found in Bharata's *Natyasastra*, a work on art in general and dramaturgy in particular. Not only in this but in many other works of aesthetics, the word *rasa* is used. The first extant work in which *rasa* has been used in an aesthetic context and with an aesthetic purpose is *Natyasastra*.

Bharata talks of *rasa*, only in the context of plays. It is not really a part of its main subject. But what he says about *rasa* implies that it is necessary not only to drama but to all forms of art.

In an off-hand manner, Bharata says that without *rasa* there can be no drama, that it is the soul of any play (*Natyasastra*, VI – 31).

As Bharata says that first of all it is necessary to explain what are *rasas*. For without *rasa* no topic (or drama) can appeal to the mind of the spectator.

It is immediately noticeable that the great emphasis laid upon the relation of *rasa* to drama—it is indispensable, says Bharata, for without it nothing 'can appeal'.

What can be deemed one of the most important qualities of any literature, any work of art? What is that element which attracts, draws attention to itself. In Indian tradition, this is not enough. Beyond the mere act of drawing attention to itself, a work of art must appeal. In other words, it should not contain mere shock value. A lot of things came into vogue and then they are forgotten. Such things might immediately catch our attention.

But they fail to sustain our attention for long. After the initial impact they may not have anything that touches us. Thus a work of art is successful only when there is appeal. Without *rasa*, according to Bharata, there can be no appeal. Hence, without *rasa*, a work of art (here, drama) is incomplete, unfulfilled.

## WHAT IS *RASA* MADE OF?

Now, the question arises that what is this *rasa* made of? What does it consists of? Bharata says in *Natyasastra* (VI. 31):

> *Rasa* is accomplished as the result of the conjunction of *Vibhava, Anubhava* and *Vyabhicharibhava* (*Bhava* is also included). All these are primarily bound up with dominant emotions, i.e. *Sthayibhava*.
>
> Giving an illustration, Bharata, in the same passage, says: Just as flavour comes from a combination of many spices, herbs and other substances, so *rasa*... from many *bhavas*.

Coming to various components or constituents that lead to *rasa*, it is already known that *rasa* is made up of such constituents as *bhavas* (*sthayibhavas, sancharibhavas* or *vyabhichari bhavas* and *sattvikbhavas*), *vibhavas* and *anubhavas*.

Earlier, Bharata has acknowledged the prior existence of *rasa* (even before it is perceived), for he says that without *rasa* no work has any meaning. Bharata claims that without *rasa* the essence of art is lost and the essence of art is aesthetic delight.

## DIFFERENT *RASAS*

As to the number of *Rasa*, Bharata acknowledged eight kinds of *Rasas* (*astaunatya rasah smrtah*) in *Natya Sastra*. But there is a controversy, that whether there are eight kinds of *rasas* or nine. His list of *Rasas* as translated into English by M.M. Ghose is as follows:

1. Erotic (*Sringara*)
2. Comic (*Hasya*)
3. Pathetic (*Karuna*)
4. Furious (*Raudra*)
5. Heroic (*Vira*)
6. Terrible (*Bhayanaka*)
7. Odious (*Bibhatsa*)
8. Marvellous (*Adbhuta*)

If, however, *Adbhuta* is the marvelous which is very minor form of sublimity, what about sublimity itself which is almost as important as Beauty. Similarly, every discerning reader would realize that *Roudra* is terror, one of the twin attitudes in tragedy associated with pity or *Bhayanak* which refers to horror. In view of this, it seems reasonable to translate *Adbhuta* as Sublimity, *Roudra* as Terrible and *Bhayanak* as Horrible. These eight *Rasas* arise out of four original ones. The Comic arises from The Erotic, The Pathetic from The Terrible, The Sublime from The Heroic and The Horrible from The Odious.

Now, we may illustrate each of them from the Western drama thus:

1. Erotic (*Sringar*): Orlando's writing love verses dedicated to his beloved Rosalind and pinning them on trees in the woods (forest) and carving them deep in the bark as described in Shakespeare's *As You Like It* or Ferdinand's playing chess with Miranda in a cave as described in Shakespeare's *The Tempest*.
2. Comic (*Hasya*): The role of Launcelot Gobbo, Shylock's servant, in Shakespeare's *The Merchant of Venice* provides sufficient material for *Hasya Rasa*.

3. Pathetic (*Karuna*) King Lear's suffering in Shakespeare's *King Lear.*
4. Terrible (*Raudra*): Catherine's anger in Shakespeare's *The Taming or the Shrew*. In *Hamlet*, young prince Hamlet's anger or of Othello's in *Othello.*
5. Heroic (*Vira*): The scene of wrestling match between the Duke's Champion Charles and Orlando in Shakespeare's *As You Like It.*
6. Horrible (*Bhayanak*): The ghost scene in Shakespeare's *Hamlet* or the scene of *Othello* where Othello strangulates Desdemona to death.
7. Odious (*Bibhatsa*): The scene in *Julius Ceasar* where Cina, the poet is torn to pieces.
8. Sublime (*Adbhuta*): The Ring episode in Shakespeare's *The Merchant of Venice.*

Here these episodes can assume the proportions of *Rasas* only when they fulfil the ingredients necessary for the manifestation of *Rasas.*

Kaudasa, Bhamaha and Dandin also recognize only eight *rasas*. Udbhata for the first time mentioned *Santa Rasa*, Rudrata added *Preyas* (the agreeable) to the number of *Rasas*. Bhoja, in his *Sarasvati-Kanthabharana*, admitted the eight *Rasas* of Bharata and added four more:

1. The Magnanimous (*Udatta*)
2. The Arrogant (*Uddhata*)
3. The Serene (*Santa*)
4. The Agreeable (*Preyas*)

He gave utmost importance to *Sringara Rasa*, and connected the four *Rasas* – the Serene, the Agreeable, the Sublime and the Arrogant with four types of characters of heroes; viz.:

| Serene (*dhir santa*) | (1) Beckets of T.S. Eliot's *Murder in the Cathedral* |
|---|---|
| | (2) Carudatta of Sudraka's *Mriksha-katika* |

| | |
|---|---|
| Romantic (*dhirlalit*) | (1) Romeo in *Romeo and Juliet* |
| | (2) Udayana of Bhasa's *Svapna Vasvadatta* |
| Vain-Glorious (*dhiroddhata*) | (1) Coriolanus |
| | (2) Bhima of Bhatta Narian's Beni, *Senhora* |
| Noble Minded or Magnanimous (*Dhiroddatta*) | (1) Prospero of *Tempest* |
| | (2) Dusyanta of Kalidasa's *Abhijnana Sakuntalam* |

Abhinavagupta made an attempt to synthesize all the *Rasas* into one *Rasa* called 'The Serene' (*Santa*). Dr. V. Raghvan supports the view of Abhinavagupta and observes: "the primordial state of mind is 'serene' what we call relish (*svada*) is one undefined state of the form of a repose of the mind, (*visrantz*). Ksemendra admitted 'the serene' as the fundamental *Rasa* (*Agni rasa*) of the *Mahabharata* and the *Ramayana*. But the *Ramayana* may also be said to contain 'the pathetic' (*karuna rasa*) as its narrative originates from the killings of a crow by the hunter leaving its mate in the utter grief and anguish, the appeal of which is profoundly evocative.

Bhavabhuti, the famour Sanskrit dramatist, considers the pathetic (*Karuna rasa*) as the basic Rasa. And in some of the lines of Shakespeare, we find the element of pathos. The following lines from *Othello* are worth quoting:

Othello: *She loved me for the dangers I had passed,*
*And I loved her that she did pity them.*

[Shakespeare's *Othello*, Act-I, Scene-III, 167-168]

Here the question arises how pathetic sentiment (*Karuna rasa*) is realized. This question, in the words of V. Raghavan, takes us straight into the greater one, "why do we see and how do we enjoy a tragedy?" It is a problem which had not yet been satisfactorily solved by Western Literary Criticism. The Western critics grappled with this problem in manifold ways. Aristotle offered a theory of Catharsis to explain the function of tragedy. Many other critics like John Denis, Rousseau, Adison and

Shopenhover formulated their theories to explain the apparent contradiction of the unpleasant in aesthetic enjoyment. The Indian way of thinking is that *Visada* or sorrow is the stable state (*sthayi-bhava*) of pathetic sentiment (*Karuna rasa*). It is the love for the person that is at the bottom of pleasure. The death of one person, whom one does not love, does *not* excite one's sorrow. Madhusudan Saraswati, Rudrabhatta and Bharata tried to explain the tragic pleasure in their own ways. But all of them agree on the point that when we see a tragic hero, we do not take him as a separate entity but a part and parcel of our own self. We consider it as ourself. Our identity is merged with his identity. In other words, at the time of seeking a pathetic scene, all egotism of the connoisseur is washed away and his mind becomes calm and tranquil. It arises above all physical barriers. Abhinavagupta holds that sorrow becomes pleasurable because it is universalized (*Sadharanikrta*). It is realized by the man who shakes off his subjectivity and acquires a state of calm contemplation, in which sorrow remains no more painful. Visvanatha holds that tears trickling down our cheeks are no proof of our grief. They may come out of our sympathy (*ardrata*). In his words: "as in the lover's pinch, in tragedy the pain is desired." It sounds like the utterance of Cleopatra:

*The stroke of death is as a lover's pinch*
*That hurts and is desired*

[Shakespeare's *Antony and Cleopatra*,
Act V, Scene II, 334-335]

Jagannatha argues that the devotees shedding of tears at the description of a deity shows that tears may not always be caused by grief. This argument is, however, not tenable because the devotees do not suffer from any pain and so there is no question of tragic pleasure in it. The Indian notion of purification of heart is analogues to Aristotle's concept of catharsis. But it would be wrong to consider catharsis as a substitute for *Rasa*. The mental state offered by catharsis in which emphasis is laid on the purification of heart through pity and terror, is basically different from the mental state offered by *Rasa*, in which pleasure reigns supreme. Moreover, catharsis refers to the psychological effect of tragedy on the audience. And as Aristotle argued, the audience is not influenced or depressed by the spectacle of suffering but in some way feels released because his subjective, potentially morbid emotions, are extended outward through pity for the tragic hero.

It is a matter of common observation that sorrow is the most sensitive of all created things. Aesthetically, tragedy does not end in catastrophe. The protagonists like the suffering that befall them. Claudis says:

> *If I must die, I will encounter darkness as a bride,*
> *And hug it in mine arms*

[Shakespeare's *Measure for Measure*,
Act-III, Sc-I, Line 84-86]

Not only Indian aesthetician has given his views about Indian aesthetics. Even Western writer has also touched this area. I.A. Richards' discussion on various occasions recall the postulates of Bhattanayaka and Abhinavagupta, the two great exponents of the *rasa-dhvani* school of Indian Poetics. Richards was convinced that an aesthetic psychology was essential for understanding appreciation and evaluation of emotions in art. Indian aesthetician always approached the issue from a psychological point of view. Paying a glowing tribute to the Indian genius, Allardyce Nicoll writes:

> This concept (i.e. *rasa*) is one that has wide application and perhaps in the West we have only lately been gropingly moving towards an appreciation of its significance. Modern aesthetic theory, with its emphasis on disinterested aesthetic contemplation, comes very close to Saskrit attitude....

The first extant treatment of aesthetic emotions in Indian poetics is by Bharata (5th C.B.C.). He envisaged the existence of some permanent, innate and latent emotions or impulses in human nature, which he called *Sthayibhavas*. He maintained: "Just as a king is supreme among men and a preceptor among his disciples, so is the *Sthayibhava* supreme among all states." These permanent states, according to him, are the basis of the *rasa* and constitute the principal theme of a poetic composition. Richards enumerates these emotions in the following terms:

> These are the names of the emotions and the emotional attitudes—anger, fear, joy, sorrow..., hope, surprise discouragement, dread... and the derivative adjectives, verbs and adverbs, enthusiastic, passionate, tender startle, delight, distress... mourning, eagerly.

Seven of Bharata's *sthayibhavas* find place in the list of modern psychology. "These impulses", says McDougall, "are the mental forces that maintain and shape all the life of individuals and societies and in them we are confronted with the central mystery of life and mind and will." In Indian poetics the states, for their vast region, are compared to an ocean. Some have called the basic state to be the root feeling, while others have likened it to the thread that holds flowers in a garland. The basic states cannot be effaced completely even by their contraries. As Bharata suggests, they are the masters of the physic region as they have many satellites.

In Indian poetics, however, the *rasa*-realisation is regarded as supreme and akin to the bliss obtainable from realization of God (*brahamanand asahodara*). Abhinavagupta has clearly pointed out that ordinary experiences circumscribe our personality, while aesthetic experience sublimates it by removal of all spatio-temporal limitations. This would explain why an actual love-affair does not produce an aesthetic experience while a poetic description does. In the hands of Abhinavgupta the *rasa* theory attains the dimensions of meta-perception. To Vishvanatha, aesthetic experience is nothing less than the relishing of one's own blissful self. "Only the cultured and passionate can relish the *rasa* of the competition; those devoid of these qualities are like the wood work, the walls and stones of the theatre." He again maintains:

> People may experience sorrow and joy from situations so far as they belong to this work-a-day world, but pleasure alone is produced from them when they are delineated in poetry and attain the position of hyper-physical existence; there is nothing illogical about this phenomena.

This difference in approaches of Indian aestheticians and Richards is notable. Most of the divergences originate from it.

As Gnoli suggests, "Aesthetic experience is ... the act of tasting of this *rasa*, of immersing oneself in it to the exclusion of all else." A detailed psychological delineation of aesthetic realization is probably India's greatest contribution to aesthetics. Compared to Indian scholars' theoretical postulates, Richards' views on this issue appear sketchy and tentative. Richards' concept of aesthetic emotion, which he calls sentiments, is contained in the following passage:

> A sentiment in his (the psychologists) terminology is not an experience in the way that an emotion, a pain, the sight of something, an image, and a thought are experiences. It is not a monetary thing but a more or less permanent arrangement in the mind; a group of tendencies towards certain thoughts and emotions organized around a central object... A sentiment, in brief, is a persisting, organizing system of dispositions.

Richards' views reveal similarities with these of Abhinavagupta on the one hand and with those of Bhattanayaka on the other. Bhattanayaka postulated three functions of words in poetry, viz. *Abhida, Bhavaktva,* and *Bhojakatva*. These are the powers of generalization, through which the aesthetic emotion is grasped in a universal way.

The psychological aesthetics of Richards, which seems to be closely akin to Bhattanayaka's suffers from dualism. But a dualist approach to *rasa* is found right from Bharata to Bhattanayaka. Even Abhinavagupta did not treat aesthetic emotion and its relish as two different things.

The Indian aestheticians have again and again highlighted the identity of sensibility of the reader with that of the creative writer.

The process of aesthetic appreciation, according to Indian aestheticians, comprises three distinct but interrelated stages: The mind of the responsive reader first becomes attuned to the emotional situation portrayed through objective correlatives (*hrdyasamvada*); it is then completely absorbed in its delineation (*tanmayibhavana*) of the aesthetic emotion; and this absorption finally results in the enjoyment of an aesthetic emotion. As

Hirnanna rightly observes, "It is this transcending of self-consciousness, this migrating from our narrow self, ... that constitutes the secret of aesthetic delight." The whole of Indian discussion on aesthetic problems hinges on this very concept of the *Sahrdaya* enjoyment of *rasa*. Not only in their general attitudes to aesthetic response but also in certain subtle aspects of the process, there is a remarkable similarity between the views of Richards and those of Indian aestheticians.

Richards is an aesthetic theorist who tries to solve the problems of art and beauty with the detachment of a scientist. Aesthetics is reckoned as the 'study of beauty'. Aesthetics cannot create objects of artistic beauty; it can only explain the norms of beauty in art-works already created by a poet or an artist. Richards is a true aesthete because he has real love for the understanding of what is beautiful in literature. It is to be noted that the critical credo of I.A. Richards has close correspondence with the Rasa theory. In its broad compass, provides close analysis of poetry, reader, poetic experience, communication, imagination, and such other subjects as are related to literature. Richards' literary criticism invites us to study these problems of literature from a psychological angle. It is a fruitful line of investigation to trace out some parallelisms between Richards' critical formulations and the Indian theory of *Rasa*, more so, because the questions raised by Richards and the solutions suggested are not very different from those of the classical Sanskrit critics. The Sanskrit scholars went into the details of almost all the important issues of literature and they divided their problems into segments too subtle and minute to be observed by a non-serious reader. But their broad critical principles are comprehensible enough and remind us again and again of the critical theories put forward by Richards and other modern critics.

The importance of comparative aesthetics is self-evident. "We study foreign literature to enrich our own, to participate more fully in the true life of the thinking world, and to strengthen the ties of common understanding."

India produced a galaxy of first rate critics. Critics like Bharata, Anadavardhan, Rajasekhara, Abhinavagupta, Kuntaka,

Bhoja, Mammata and in recent years. S. Kuppuswami, Sastri, V.A. Ramaswami, P.V. Kane, V. Raghavan, S.K. De, Krishna Chaitanya etc. are the gems of world literature. All of them differ in their techniques which is a natural thing but the basic question posed by them and the solutions arrived by them are common. It is a fact that peculiarities of sensibility and outlook separate the East from the West. But the gulf can be bridged and the twin may meet. The new consciousness which has now started growing is almost compelling several Indians to look at British literature through Indian eyes. This argues well for the future of both India and England. It is not true that whatever is old is always correct. Nor is it true that whatever is new is always false. Unless we avoid these extremes and prepare ourselves for a new reconciliation, we cannot judge either our own literature or the Western literature impartially. And an intimate knowledge of the two literatures alone can produce an awakening and enrichment of what may be called world-consciousness. The Indian method of treatment is aphoristic i.e., *Sutra Saili* or *Samasa Saili* as contrasted with the Western method of treatment, which is elucidatory, i.e. *Vyasa Saili* or *Vyakhyatmaka Saili.*

It has been now universally acknowledged that in India there has been a pretty rich and long tradition of literary criticism. The depth and variety of Sanskrit literature have been widely recognized. In view of this, it is a pity that we should turn to Western literature only in order to appraise the worth of our own literary output. Sanskrit critics were endowed with great talent and there is hardly any literary problem, which is left untouched by them. It is thus proper that we should feel grateful to those ancient classical critics for bequeathing to us such an abundant variety of critical literature which can stand us in good stead even now.

From the discussion in the foregoing pages it can be well conceived that the principles of aesthetics as evolved in India are of much deeper significance than those evolved in the West. As noted above India contributed a fully developed philosophy of aesthetics whereas in the West these have been aestheticians but no composite body of philosophy could evolve. There have been no doubt individual viewpoints regarding aspects of aesthetic consideration. Therefore, we should hold the Indian principles of aesthetics as the standard and apply them to works of art to assess their aesthetic merit.

It is important to note that tragedy does not find any mention in Bharata's *Natya Sastra* and further in elaboration of the theory of *rasa* because the whole concept is related to the philosophy of life that the ultimate goal of life is to find peace and happiness. Since that is the goal, sorrow, pain or suffering are only stations in the journey of life and they have to be considered as part of the whole stream of life. They cannot be viewed in isolation but if done so they will result in giving a distorted picture of life sufficient enough to mislead any man. Life therefore has to be viewed, as one whole and if any part is to be examined it will be only in relation to the whole.

## REFERENCES

Gupteshwar Prasad, *I.A. Richards and Indian Theory of Rasa.*

H.L. Sharma, *Indian Aesthetic and Aesthetic Perspective.*

Priyadarshani Patnaik, *Rasa in Aesthetic.*

R.S. Singh, *The Poetics of I.A. Richards: A Collection of Critical Essays.*

# *Silence! The Court is in Session*: A Strong Social Commentary

4

*Shubha Tiwari*

Vijay Tendulkar is known for his concern for burning social problems and anomalies of Indian society and mindset. *Silence! The Court is in Session* is one of his most famous and widely appreciated plays. A group of actors are enacting a mock-drama, actually a mock trial of Ms Benare. The pettiness of conversation among actors suggests that drama-activity has cheapened itself quite a lot in recent times in India. There is no seriousness, no gravity, and no mutual respect among actors. Drama is basically an intellectual activity. It needs committed people. It needs talented and serious people. But here we find that the actors are busy jeering at each other. They want to expose and humiliate each other. Their way of 'passing time' is cheap indeed.

During the first half of the play, Benare is able to outsmart them. She is not caught in their net. Her voice is not throttled. But the later half of the play witnesses a mock trial of Benare that is actually a trial of the whole female race in this country. It shows our hypocrisy, our double standards regarding men and women. Benare is accused of cheap conduct, of wooing men, of fulfilling her bodily needs and so on and so forth. But the intellectual, the absent university professor, Damle who is equally a part of the bad conduct, is not at all held responsible. The very fact that he does not turn up speaks for his sense of responsibility towards this stained woman, Benare.

Kumud Mehta writes well, 'The door latch has long since fallen into place. The group has by now safely insulated itself. What began as a game has evolved into a hunt. Benare is the quarry and the group, accuser and judge, rolled into one. The sentence meted out to her is savage: the infant in her womb must be destroyed; she must lose her teaching job, her only source of livelihood. There is no mention of the intellectual who abandoned her, the absent Damle.

Having created this situation, the playwright seems to have had no other option except to allow Benare her say. Her inner frame stirs a little to communicate to us what she knows about men who profess love but, in fact, only hunger for the flesh.' (VI)

Society is at its best, most natural and relaxed ground censoring 'bad' women as though there existed 'bad' women without 'bad' men. The whole responsibility of morally upright behaviour is bulldozed on women. Men are, by nature, considered to be willful, wild, childish, innocent and mischievous. Their sins are no sins at all. The society has a very light, parental, and pampering sort of attitude when it comes to sexual offences of men. In case of women, the iron rod gets hot and hotter. No punishment is actually enough for such a woman. There is no respite, no shade, and no soothing cushion for a sinning woman. She must be stained and abandoned. Her femininity, her needs, her very existence must be ignored, or rather destroyed. She must be cornered and brutally killed—both in physical and psychological senses.

The play is about the pathetic position of women in the male-dominated Indian world. All philanthropic assumptions of human nature have been thoroughly butchered. The play poignantly portrays the plight, the ponderings, predicaments and problems of a middle class Indian woman. Society as a force is hostile to individual instincts as well as dignity. The very system of justice is gender-biased.

Leela Benare is an actress in an amateur drama troupe. The beginning of her exploitation begins with her uncle who had exploited her sexually in her teen age. The question of marrying her did not arise for him. To top the torture, even her own mother fails to understand her and support her. But Benare shows guts. She starts her life all over again, studies and finally settles into a teaching job. As a teacher, she comes in contact with Prof. Damle whom she considers quite intelligent, and academically bright. Though married, the Professor exploits her sexually and naturally refuses to marry her. As she is pregnant with the Professor's child, she is desperate to find a way to escape social wrath and humiliation. She requests two of her colleagues at the drama company to marry her. But obviously enough, they are more smart. They also refuse to attach their names with her. The bitter experiences of life embitter her tongue like anything. Like the playwright himself, Benare is also very vocal, very open and frank in her attack on male chauvinism and false concepts of masculinity. To pay her back in the same coin, the actors plan to expose and humiliate her through a mock trial. She gets into the trap. Once the trial begins, there is no shelter for poor Benare. She is labelled by all dirty adjectives. Prof. Damle has been spared the iron rod. It is Benare who is accused of immorality, sin, promiscuity, over-sexuality and so on and so forth. The verdict dismisses her from her school job, orders for abortion, and blackens Leela Benare's name forever.

The problem with Leela Benare is that she is too much of a woman. She is sexually alive. She needs to fulfill her desires. And above everything else, she is not ashamed of her instincts. She is not submissive. She does not fit into the wrapper society has so meticulously prepared for its women over centuries of patriarchal thinking. She too could have carried out all her sexual escapades secretly and would have maintained a damsel-like, falsely innocent demeanor. But she does not do it. She does something and accepts it, 'My life is my own – I haven't sold it to anyone for a job! My will is my own. My wishes are my own. No one can kill those – no one.' (SC 58)

The society cannot forgive such candid attitudes. Benare feels that it is not she who is defiling the noble teaching profession; it is people like hypocritical Damle who do not deserve to be called teachers. They may or may not be great scholars but their actual conduct is worm-like, cheap and animal-like. They do not have the courage to accept an act they have performed; they cannot bear the responsibility attached to romantic liaisons. They are cowards. For them, women are just flesh. Women are to be used, stained forever and then thrown away. The significant presence in the play is the absence of

Damle. It is as though the woman has got pregnant all by herself; the male counterpart has no role, no responsibility in the matter.

The play exactly describes middle class mentality and its pettiness. The theatre members are a bored, frustrated, and repressed lot. Their attitude towards their fellow beings is hostile, malicious, and spiteful. They are mediocre and the bond of mediocrity gets very strong in the presence of an antagonistical force named Leela Benare. She is lively. She ignores society and its trivial, hypocritical norms. This is enough to isolate her from the rest of the lot. She is targeted and finally defeated.

The President of the drama group is Mr. Kashikar. He is always seen with his wife. The duo of this husband-wife reminds one of Mamapapa in Anita Desai's *Fasting, Feasting*. The couple is a super hypocrite, leading a false life that is devoid of any meaning. Tendulkar brings out the hollowness of their life so well. Mr. Kashikar buys flowers for wife. Mrs. Kashikar buys shirts for husband. They make a constant show of fondness in public. Their perpetual show of love becomes distasteful and repulsive. Mr. Kashikar, a male chauvinist, does not let the wife speak at all. Whenever she tries to give an opinion, hubby dear promptly shuts her up. But the problem is that Benare ruthlessly unravels their pettiness before their own eyes. She is very direct in her words. She plainly tells that they have adopted a boy in order to lessen the monotony of their lives. They have deprived that child of a separate identity and maturity. What Benare says is true and therefore it is bitter. Once the play within the play (the mock trial) begins, Tendulkar brilliantly dissects and shows the sick psyche of urban middle class society in India. The double standards are sickening. On one hand, there is this woman who is trying to hold her head high in the face of social humiliation. On the other hand, there are these sadistic members of the drama company whose only pleasure lies in exposing, torturing and laughing at the cornered woman.

Each artist represents an unfulfilled dream. Boredom pervades their lives. Sukhatme is quite inefficient as a lawyer. Mr. and Mrs. Kashikar are childless. Ponkshe fails to become a scientist. Karnik is a failure as an actor. Rokde does not have an identity of his own. This petty lot finds in Benare a suitable enemy. But amongst themselves even, they do not have anything but hatred for each other. Every uttering has a dual meaning for them. Even innocent remarks are taken as sexually loaded ones. These perverted people want to mentally replay the sexual encounters of Benare. They want to derive pleasure out of this crooked means. Playing with anyone's emotions, or peeping into the private affairs of a person—these things are quite common and accepted for them.

The behavioral case that society has created for a woman is very congested, tight, suffocating and rigid. A woman must not be free. She must not laugh loudly. She must not enjoy life. Mrs. Kashikar, in particular, is very harsh on Benare, 'That's what happens these days when you get everything without marrying. They just want comfort. Just look at the way she behaves. I don't like to say anything since she's one of us. Should there be no limit to how freely a woman can behave with a man? An unmarried woman? Look how loudly she laughs! How she sings, dances, cracks jokes! And wandering alone with how many men, day in and day out!' (SC 99-100)

The inherent mentality behind these words has been shaped by centuries of patriarchy wherein pleasure is considered to be the sole domain of males. A woman who enjoys sex is something odd and dirty. Women are either 'devis' or devils. The society does not accept women as normal human beings who have vices as well as well virtues.

The very word 'life' gives a pang of joy. To live is life. To sing, to feel, to experiment, to enjoy, to dance, to breathe, to travel, to know, to explore—all this is life. But when you do all this, the society labels you as 'evil' and gives a verdict that hangs you. This is the paradox of life—to live and not to live—'Life is like this. Life is so and so. Life is such and such. Life is a book that goes ripping into pieces. Life is a poisonous snake that bites itself. Life is a betrayal. Life is a fraud. Life is a drug. Life is drudgery. Life is a something that's nothing or a nothing that's something... Milord, life is a dreadful thing. Life must be hanged... Life is not worthy of life. Hold an enquiry against life. Sack it from its job.' (SC 116)

At a deeper level, the play is a comment on lack of individual importance in life, the meaninglessness of life, and the absurdity of various human situations. In philosophical terms, this play is a blow to all those who seek meaning out of this mundane, bizarre, ordinary human existence. To live is to be 'exuberant' and 'exuberant' one is not allowed to be. How often we meet parents who teach their children to laugh mildly. Everyone is scared of being wild. And wildness is part and parcel of human nature. Socializing in this sense means living coyly and submissively. Life becomes death. The society compels one to live less and less. It forces one to live not life but death itself. This sort of life gives birth to all sorts of anomalies. We see abnormal people all around with 'so sweet' faces but complex, pervert's minds.

'These are the mortal remains of some cultured men of twentieth century. See their faces – how ferocious they look. Their lips are full of lovely worn out phrases! And their bellies are full of unsatisfied desires.' (SC 117)

How true these comments are for contemporary men! Every man is a wolf wrapped in the skin of a lamb. He wants his 'pound of flesh'. For him, every woman is virtually her body – bones, flesh, curves! A woman is not identified with her intellect, her ability, her intelligence, her courage or knowledge. A woman, whosoever she may be, is just her body. Even women themselves have internalized this vision about themselves. They see their own selves as bodies. That is why they are afraid and ashamed of old age, wrinkles and white hairs. They view themselves primarily as sex objects. This is what patriarchy has done to women – poisoned their self-perception beyond repair.

Leela Benare is mercifully different. But difference and deviation are things Indian society does not give to its women. So Leela Benare pays the price of being different.

## REFERENCES

Vijay Tendulkar. 1995. *Five Plays*. Delhi: OUP.

Vijay Tendulkar. 2002. *Silence! The Court is in Session*. Delhi: OUP.

# Social Satire and Realistic Themes in Nissim Ezekiel's 'Three Plays'

5

*Dipika Sahai*

The *Three Plays* of Nissim Ezekiel are a sarcasm on the so-called liberal, modern, advanced men and women of progressive India. The first play *Nalini* is a wry commentary on the current art scene in India. The second *Marriage Poem* is a one Act tragi-comedy – more a comedy than tragedy which depicts "the light and shade that comprise the social institution called marriage."[1] The third play *The Sleepwalkers* is also a One-Act play in which Ezekiel has shown the depravity of the so-called elite of today who still look up to Americans visiting India. Ezekiel's plays provide healthy social criticism with exquisite touches of irony and satire.

*Nalini* is a comedy about the painter Nalini, and the two advertising executives Raj and Bharat who have their ulterior motives. They want to work for the publicity of the exhibition of Nalini's paintings so that they can come close to her and are able to exploit her. The play is a scathing attack on the artists who have become commercial rather than remaining pure artists, and also on art critics who have no knowledge about art. For them there is no difference between Roger Fry and Christopher Fry. The theme is realistic and the play holds a mirror up to the vulgarity of the so-called intellectuals. Ezekiel speaks through his characters who have double personalities: their public life and inner life. He had observed these people from very close when he worked as an art critic in *Times of India*. As such he was familiar with the exhibitions of painters and had a very good understanding of their personal and public affairs. He had been a manager for some time in Shilpi Advertising, a Sarabhai concern. So he knew very well about the slick world of business executives and also about the intellectual dishonesty of these executives.

The play opens with clear and specific stage directions, with Bharat listening to soft, quiet classical music in a room adorned with books and colourful paintings. Raj enters and asks his friend Bharat to arrange for the publicity of the exhibition of Nalini's paintings. The play, as we know, is a social satire on mere glitter, pomp and show of modernity. It is a sarcasm on modern artists who feel that their art is not sufficient in itself to be praised, it needs publicity. So the first priority of the artist today is publicity. Raj tells Bharat:

> "I'm sure she is very particular about the publicity. She intends to organise that first. She probably has a few paintings ready. The others she could paint in due course. She has booked the gallery."[2] (10)

It is not the quality of painting that matters but the right contacts. Raj says:

> "Help me to plan the publicity for Nalini's exhibition. You have some influence with the journalists, contacts in the right places... You dine with them, you drink with them. That's important. Nalini probably has some photographs of herself, with her paintings in the background... Holding a brush in her hand." (11)

Since Nalani is pretty Raj wants to win her favour, and Bharat knows that:

> "BHARAT: And you're going to handle the publicity for this exhibition in exchange for Nalini's kisses... and all that." (11)

The exhibition is a vehicle for coming closer to Nalini. These two friends are no art critics in the real sense of the word, have no idea about the art of painting, but thrive on contacts alone. When Bharat asks whether Nalini's paintings are worth exhibiting Raj retorts:

> "Does that matter? They are paintings, canvases with colour on them, plenty of colour in various forms. They don't represent anything, I guess. They are just paintings." (11)

Throughout the play Ezekiel is sarcastic about these art critics. They do not want to criticise and lose a friend, hence they indulge in false praise. They know the truth about themselves:

> "BHARAT: Who are we to criticise, anyway? What do we understand about painting?" (13)

There are ironical remarks in the play on art critics who judge a painting not on its creativity or its shades and colours but its photographs. Bharat says:

> "If she brings some photographs of her paintings, I'll know what to write about them." (14)

The technique of advertising is attacked. It is not art which is promoted these days but people, art is only a via medium. Bharat says:

> "...what does it matter whether Nalini's paintings are goods or not? They are paintings, and I have the reputation of one who encourages artists... Let's decide how I'm going to help promote Nalini as an artist, promote you with her, promote myself with her." (15)

Bharat confesses to Nalini that he does not understand painting at all but has become an art critic because he had nothing else to do and that:

> "...there's prestige in art, intellectual respectability and all that. It's the same with the theatre, dance, music, all the arts... I got into art by accident ...Now I've been in it for ten years, And I like being in it, I honestly do. It's fun." (33)

Ezekiel condemns art critics who have no idea of art but are only snobs. Bharat says:

> "I can't build anything. I can't create anything. I can mix only with others like me, who dress like me, talk like me, live like me. So I work in an advertising agency. The pay is good, and everybody in the profession dresses well. I can't stand people who don't dress well." (35)

It is a sarcasm on modern executives who are lost in their image of being well dressed, but cannot involve themselves in the world around. They lack a sense of commitment. They will have to commit themselves to something more than their comforts and pleasures.

The characters in the play are types. We can meet them anywhere in urban India. Ezekiel has portrayed the shallow world of business executives, a world of pretence. Bharat is glad to know that in the changed India not all women are rigid about morals:

> "For most of us abroad it only means encounters with women. That kind of freedom and adventure and experience I have here, the way our women are progressing... Angela goes to church but she's not altogether... unco-operative. She understands a litle bit about what men need, and women too." (14)

He is cynical about women and their modernity – the new Indian women who are not Sitas and Savitris.

Ezekiel is intolerant of people going abroad for false reputation. He makes a fun of them when Raj says:

> "You could go abroad and come back. They make better use of you when you go abroad and come back. At least they pay you better. You need not learn anything abroad. Just go and come back." (13)

He is bitter with the female writers who

> "...write only middles for The Times of India and articles about their foreign junkets and intimate revelations about their quarrels with their husbands and difficulties with their children." (13)

He has no soft corner for men and women who take undue advantage in the name of 'freedom', 'adventure' and 'experience.' One has to understand that "liberty is not licence." (21) It is an attack on the concept of modernity when Bharat says:

> "I'm perfectly capable of acting without thinking... We are the busy, active men of the city. We are all in good jobs... We read good books – foreign books, of course... We don't make loud, gurgling sounds when we drink our tea or

soup... Our marriages are not arranged for us... We are not communalistic, provincial or parochial." (16)

Modern man is advanced only as it suits him. He is callous, cannot fight orthodoxy and tyranny. "He is Indian by accident of birth," (17) as Bharat says. Today we make a wrong use of the word 'intellectual' when we want to avoid a discussion we say "I am not an intellectual." (17) The word 'intellectual' is used by Ezekiel as if it were an accusation. Bharat says:

"If I tell you, you will accuse me of being an intellectual." (20)

Bharat's frequent references to himself as an intellectual are a satire on his false notions about himself. As a modern man he is living in an illusion. He does not want to listen to the voices of conscience which trouble him all the time. He is living in a make-shift world. The voice of conscience is always honest, but in this transitional world one cannot afford to listen to it. Not listening to conscience is like crushing one's soul. Bharat is a snob who thinks we should act first and then think. He is totally exposed in the enactment of his fantasy about his dream girl Nalini and his advances to her. But when she appears as a person in reality and snubs him, he is shocked. Nalini fires Bharat:

"...you're incapable of being truthful... But you just can't help shooting a line at me, hoping for the best. You're essentially a gambler." (37)

Men are often prejudiced against women artists. They generalize all women in one category. But, Nalini says, even they have their individual qualities:

"You have a formula; you can't imagine an individual woman. You can't believe that a woman may want to create a world of her own just as a creative man does, a woman with the will to explore herself and the world around her." (38)

In the words of K.R.S. Iyengar "Nalini has a double personality of the artist, half-woman half omniscient with the eyes of God, and thus isolated from humanity."[3] She explains the creative process to Bharat. According to Nalini, every piece of art involves creativity: the whole personality of the artist is transformed:

> "Gradually I began to understand that what I did to colour and form and composition was also being done to myself. Everytime I created a painting, I created myself. I could not remain what I was. I had to change." (40)

The artist is compared to God. Nalini tells us that after she had finished painting the final product was very different from anything she had in mind:

> "There was noting but chaos before me. But soon the chaos was clarified, the forms emerged distinct and transparent. I saw in the painting what my eyes had never seen in life or in art." (41)

Real art is inspiration, depth and intensity on the part of the artist. When the creation comes into being then only the artist realizes the true meaning of joy. Nalini says:

> "I had experienced myself dividing into two persons... one person was the woman I am, the other person was... another person... [who] suffered from some unimaginable upheaval within her. She was alone, separated from humanity." (41)

She differentiates between the man who experiences and the artist who is inspired and creates. She talks about the other person, the artist as:

> "She saw the world in a different way, not with my eyes... definitely not with my eyes... With the eyes of God." (41)

Just like God the artist creates the future. Nalini's vision of an artist is that he enjoys the freedom to create something new. Future is created from exploration and that is the evolution of the artist. Nalini is a true artist who does not succumb to the pressures of such art critics as Raj and Bharat.

In *Nalini* Ezekiel has presented the unusual human predicament of today. He has given a contrast between life and art. Modern man is trapped. He can only pursue thought but will not act. Life has become stagnant, whereas art explores, discovers, invents. Life is dull. Even when we change it is not in the real sense. It is only:

> "Another drink, another girl, another party, another sales conference, another exhibition..." (47)

On the contrary art has a future for all as Bharat asserts after listening to Nalini:

> "It's a sort of vision you have." (43)

At the end of the play Ezekiel shows the mirror to modern man when Bharat says:

> "But when I look into a mirror, I see only one man, myself. I see him drinking and talking... And I can't believe in this man... He is too insubstantial. Almost a ghost... He only advances his own self-interest. For that he works really hard. In everything else – politics, culture, personal relations, professional concern, civil matters, everything, he is basically frivolous. Even when he talks seriously, he is frivolous." (47-8)

Bharat sees a ghost in the image of man who advances his own self-interest, whereas for Nalini, the artist creates a now world out of chaos, like God. But this second Nalini is yet to be born.

Ezekiel has made his sarcasm more poignant by contrasting Bharat, the executive with Nalini, the genuine artist.

The second play *Marriage Poem* is full of wit and humour. Mala is shown as a possessive wife and Naresh a flirting husband. Naresh lives in the world of fantasy and makes love to Leela.

The play is a satire on the institution of marriage itself which requires trust, love and honesty on part of both the partners. Mala is greatly disturbed by the flirtations of her husband and seeks the advice of Mrs. Lall.

"MALA: What would you do if your husband became attached to another woman?

Mrs. Lall: ...I would make a terrible fuss. I would harass my husband night and day till he gave her up... I would behave like a mad woman... I would tear my hair and I would tear his hair... I'll write to all the papers. I'll complain to the Home Minister. What's the use of being Home Minister if he can't guarantee the sanctity of the home? I'll take out a procession and shout slogans against him. We'll gherao the other woman." (65)

Mrs. Lall's reply is the best comedy one can imagine. Even the stage-direction is superb:

"Spectacular music, military or similar, to parody the aggressive speech just made." (65)

The theme of the play is realistic with subtle comments and interesting witty dialogues. Ezekiel shows how foolishly people behave in these situations and make themselves a laughing stock. The sarcasm will be more evident when the play is enacted on the stage rather than in reading. The dialogues are crisp and witty. Chetan Karnani has commented, "In the brilliant combination of dream and reality Naresh looks like the married version of Bharat." (121)

The third play *Sleepwalkers* is "a hilarious, rollicking farce."[4] (121) It is a one Act play built on the theme "Give us this day our daily American." (83) The play begins and ends with this chant. Indian guests have collected at a Reception party for an American couple in an American home in India. The Indian guests are in masks because these characters are 'types' and not individuals as Ezekiel would like to have them for the audience. He finds it really disgusting, the servile way in which the Indians compromise their self-respect on seeing people from America.

Mr. Morris and Mrs. Morris have come to India to launch their magazine 'Blank', so that it may enable people to dispense with thinking altogether. Even the title of the magazine is significant. Mr. Morris says: "We discourage ideas" (90); the response to it shows the hollowness of the guests who are stupefied:

"MR. VARMA: My stories are perfectly suitable for your magazine, Mr. Morris. My critics say that they are totally without thought.

MISS GANGULI: This will be a very good thing for Bengal. People think too much there. That's why all this stone-throwing and burning of buses. If we had less thinking we could have stable Government.

MR. KAPUR: A magazine without thought will be popular with Indian women, Mrs. Morris. We get along peacefully without thought.

PROF. SHAH: In this country, Mr. Morris, the ideal of many of us is to transcend thought, to reach a state of mind where thought is unnecessary." (90)

There are amusing situations and dialogues replete with humour. The pseudo-civilized society of modern India where we talk of equal status to women is ridiculed:

"MRS. RAMAN: O no, our husbands drink whisky, we drink orange juice.

MRS. KAPUR: Our husbands eat meat. We eat vegetables.

PROF. SHAH: This is division of labour." (86)

There is a great sarcasm on the teaching profession too:

"MR. MORRIS: You combine teaching and writing, don't you, Prof. Shah? you must find teaching takes up a lot of your time.

PROF. SHAH: Only the mornings, Mr. Morris. My afternoons and evenings are free... My lectures were all prepared twenty years ago... The notes I prepared as a student, Mr. Morris twenty years ago, I use those." (92-3)

The programme of culture and economic exchange between India and America is also satirised:

"PROF. SHAH: We give you spiritual aid, you give us financial aid.

MR. MORRIS: ...Fair exchange is no robbery.

MISS GANGULI: ...You give us Hemingway, we give you Rabindranath Tagore." (88)

The most interesting episode is the reply of Miss Ganguli when she is questioned about the theme of her plays. She writes on Family Planning. When Mr. Morris asks her whether the villagers are convinced about Family Planning after seeing the plays, Miss Ganguli replies that they are convinced but they cannot do anything about it.

"MISS GANGULI: ....We are five hundred million, and most of us in the villages, and there's no entertainment in the villages or anything like that. You know, the way you have night clubs and so on." (94)

Mr. Morris asks Mr. Raman:

"MR. MORRIS: ...Would the Government of India permit an American foundation to set up night clubs in Indian villages?

MR. RAMAN: I don't know anything about that, Mr. Morris. I specialise in reporting strikes, protests, processions, and so on." (94)

In the *Three Plays* Ezekiel laughs at the characters and through them at the world around him. At times he reminds us of Bernard Shaw[5] as in the comments on women and persons who are self-conscious about their intellect as when Bharat says:

> "Pascal says that the sum of evil in the world would be much diminished if men could only learn to sit quietly in their rooms. I am busy diminishing the sum of evil in the world." (9)

## NOTES

1. Chetan Karnani, *Nissim Ezekiel* (New Delhi: Arnold Heinemann, 1974), p. 118.
2. Nissim Ezekiel, *Three Plays* (A Writers Workshop Bluebird Book), p. 10. All subsequent references are from this edition.
3. K.R. Srinivas Iyengar, *Indian writing in English* (New Delhi: Sterling Publishers Private Limited, 2003), p. 731.
4. Karnani, p. 121.
5. Ibid., pp. 113-14.

# *Ghasiram Kotwal*: A Study in the Politics of Power and Revenge

6

*Ashok Kumar Sharma*

Vijay Tendulkar is a significant name amongst the contemporary Marathi playwrights. In the modern India, Parsi, Marathi, Gujrati theatres are the oldest. But the fact remains playwriting in India has not been prolific and of high order. Most of the plays have been written for reading and not for staging. Some playwrights have simply imitated and some have adapted to Indian situations, the Western plays. Some significant playwrights of the present time come from different regions such as Girish Karnad, Badal Sirkar, Vijay Tendulkar and Mohan Rakesh. They represent different regions and they have written plays in vernacular languages viz. – Kannada, Bangla, Marathi and Hindi.

Vijay Tendulkar (b–1928) has been a front runner among the avante-garde playwrights. He has written till date 30 full length plays, 23 one act plays. He has written screen plays for eight Marathi movies. He has written for popular movies such as Saamna 1975 (Confrontation), Simhasan 1979 (The Throne) and Umbartha 1981 (The Threshold). Recently Vijay Tendulkar Festival was organized in Oct 2004 in New York by Indo-American Art Council. He has been called a literary journalist, humanist and a social critic by the I.A.C.C.

*Sakharam Binder* (1972), *Ghasiram Kotwal* (1972) and *Kamala* (1981) are Tendulkar's such plays which deal with sex and violence. The impact of the twin human instincts on social fabric has been the prime concern of the playwright. *Ghasiram Kotwal* has its source in history, deal with power politics and has been presented through music, dance and chorus. Sutradhar as commentator and character also plays a very vital role. Balaji Janardan Banu Phadnavis a historical figure as ruler,

Pune as the centre and lust and revenge as the evils occupy the prominent place in it.

*Sakharam Binder* (1972) is the story of a man who loves physical pleasure. For him women are the pleasure toys. Sakharam Binder is a study in masochism. In another play *Kamala* (81), which deals with an actual journalistic story as its source, exposes the rural flesh trade. Veena Noble Dass is apt when she says:

> The plays 'Shantata Court Chaloo Aahe' (Silence ! The Court is in Session), 'Giddh' (Vultures), 'Sakharam Binder' and 'Ghasiram Kotwal' which made Tendulkar a popular playwright, are experiments of an intense and deeper impulse and not just a matter of superficial innovation.[1]

Moreover, in the above discussed plays women are at the receiving ends. They suffer at the hands of man. Hence, these plays have been called gyno-centric. In *Sakharam Binder*, *Giddh* and *Ghasiram Kotwal*, we notice sex and violence. "The phrase sex and violence is very loosely attributed to in the discussion of these plays. But in none of these, the theme of sex and violence is superficial, as it forms an important part of the content of the plays."[2]

The abiding popularity of *Ghasiram Kotwal* is for two reasons. First it deals with politics as a game of power. Secondly it deals with the evils related with power politics, the play has attracted a large number of spectators the world over. N.S. Dharan avers in the following words:

> The inescapable reality is that as long as politics remains a power game Phadnavis, Ghasirams, and Lalta Gauris are bound to emerge. Not only in India but the world over, we witness, Ghasiram Kotwals being played on real political theaters. This universal political reality in fact accounts for the abiding popularity of the play.[3]

As told above it is based on a historical incident taken from the life of Balaji Janardan Banu Peshwas' Phadnavis of Pune. He was a shrewd politician who succeeded in keeping Britishers away from the Maratha empire. He was a hero worshiped by Marathas. But Tendulkar chose a shady side of his character in which he made Ghasiram Sawaldas the Kotwal of Pune in exchange of his daughter Lalita Gauri. The playwright focuses on this shady aspect of Maratha's hero which created a great uproars in Pune where the play was first staged. The play which was staged by "Bharat Natya Mandir" Pune in Dec 1972, was stopped by the President of P.D.A. after 19 performances finding it controversial. The main reason behind the ban was:

> This deglamorization of a cult hero caused disquiet among Poonites who came down heavily upon the producer, director and actors of the play.[4]

The main characters in the play are Phadnavis, Ghasiram and Lalita Gauri. Apart from it there is a 12 member Chorus and Sutradhar. Ghasiram Sawaldas is a Brahmin from Kannauj but he lives an ignoble life. He has been shown dancing with Gulabi where he meets Peshwa Phadnavis. He gives him money and necklace as gifts. But the Brahmins of Pune not only snatch money and necklace from him but also treats him cruelly which forces him to take a vow to avenge his humiliation.

"(Takes off his sash, throws it on the ground)

But I'll come back. I'll come back to Poona. I'll show my strength. It will cost you, your good days are gone ! I am a Kannauj Brahmin, but I've become a Shudra, a criminal a useless animal .......... I will make this Poona a Kingdom of pigs. Then I'll be Ghasiram again, the son of Savaldas once more."[5]

To avenge his humiliation he goes to the extent of sailing his daughter Lalita Gauri to Peshwa Phadnavis. It is a turning point in the play, which turns it into a revenge play. Generally, the reason for revenge is hurting of one's self-respect or honour or loss of love or betrayal. Draupadi's taking oath in *Mahabharat* or Chanakya's taking oath to destroy the ruler of Magadh may be compared with Ghasiram Savaldas' oath. Though the play has only two Acts but it has a complex structure. As far as the basic instincts of survival and aggression are concerned the play *Ghasiram Kotwal* may be compared with *Spanish Tragedy*, *Hamlet* and *Duchess of Malfi*. Its story is rooted in 19th century Indian history. The play successfully shows lecherous, greedy and Machiavellian politician with no moral scruples. Following lines give us a glimpse of lecherous ruler who begs from his subordinate his daughter:

> Nana: Just one more time. Ghasiram. Just one more time, you bastard.[6]

The play presents contrasting characters. On the one hand we have Nana the willy and lecherous ruler. On the other hand we have Ghasiram Savaldas who wants power by any means to become an exploiterer from the state of being an exploited creature. Savaldas when becomes Kotwal he turns to his exploiterers and becomes a terror. Pune Changes overnight:

> "Prostitute's lane was desolate
> The chasing of women was halted
> Pimps turned into beggar
> Counterfeit coins were worthless."[7]

The play shows the both the characters plan to avenge their defeats. Nana wants to eliminate Ghasiram Kotwal. He secretly manipulates to get rid of him. While Ghasiram wants to release his daughter Lalita Gauri from the clutches of Nana and wants to see her married to a suitable groom. We discover at the end that the cleverer of the two finally wins. Ghasiram Kotwal emerges as a tormenter and the Brahmins of Pune rise in revolt. They seek order from Nana to behead Ghasiram. At the end he is stoned to death. Thus the play succeeds in presenting political power and revenge at their worst.

The play shows that the desire for power and the desire to settle score with one's opponents are so strong that one can touch the bottom in the creations. They easily fit in the present political scenario as well.

Another significant thing worth nothing is the presentation of sex and violence without showing it on the stage. Chorus of 12 person and Sutradhar intimate things time. And this artistic play successfully presents politics of power and revenge thought the artefacts of folk art forms. Vijay Tendulkar told in an interview to Samik Bandyopadhyay:

> 'Ghasiram' started with a theme, then came the specific story or incident which was historical and then the search for the form began. By a series of accidents I discovered the present form which is a combination of a variety of ingredients from different folk from of Maharashtra.[8]

We admit that there may be some distortions in the play. But if we take it only as a political satire or a revenge play it would certainly give us the same artistic pleasure as before because the situations and events which the play *Ghasiram Kotwal* exhibits, deal with universal human behaviour and weaknesses. And that is the greatness of the play.

## NOTES

1. Dass, Veena Noble, "Experiment and Innovation in Modern Indian Drama: In translation." Studies in contemporary Indian Drama ed. Sudhakar Pandey, Freya Taraporewala, Prestige Books, New Delhi, 1990, p. 70.
2. Ibid., p. 70.
3. Dharan, N.S., "The plays of Vijay Tendulkar", Creative Books, New Delhi, 1999, p. 100.
4. Ibid., p. 101.
5. Tendulkar, Vijay, "Ghasiram Kotwal", (3rd Printing), Seagull Books, Calcutta, 1999, pp. 26-27.
6. Ibid., p. 34.
7. Ibid., p. 38.
8. Ibid., p. 101.

# *Ghasiram Kotwal* as a Political Play

7

*Smita Mishra*

Vijay Tendulkar's *Ghasiram Kotwal*, a musical historical play set in Maharashtra of the late eighteenth century, recounts the power games played out in terms of caste ascendancy in politics. It is a dramatic exposure of the latent violence, treachery, sexuality and immorality that characterize politics. *Ghasiram Kotwal*, the play, shows a man who, caught in the matrix of opportunistic ethics of modern world, feels alienated. It shows how a common man, seeking power, confronts the people who were already in power and undergoes an organic change.

The play was first performed on 16 December 1972 at the *Bharat Natya Mandir*, Pune by the Progressive Dramatic Association of Pune. In 1972-73 it won several awards at the Maharashtra State Drama competition. However, the President of PDA banned the play after nineteen performances, citing the reasons, namely (a) it was anti-Brahmin (b) the character of Nana Phadnavis as conceived by the playwright was historically not correct and (c) there was a fear of revolt in the audience and a strong possibility that the play would be publicly abused by the audience if the performance continued. Protesting against the ban, most of the actors of PDA resigned and revived the play on 11 January 1974, and it has ever since been performed extensively both in India and abroad by the troupe.

When asked by Samik Bandyopadhyay if he really conceived the play as a study on power games or as an exposure of Brahmin corruption and pretensions. Tendulkar replied:

> Broadly speaking, I had in mind the emergence, the growth and the inevitable end of the Ghasiram, also those who create, and help Ghasiram to grow; and the irony of

stoning to death a person pretending that it is the end of Ghasirams.[1]

The information together with Tendulkar's denial that the play is historical and the following assertion, 'It is a story, in prose, verse, music and dance set in a historical era. Ghasirams are creations of socio-political forces which know no barriers of time and place'[2] suggests that he intends the play to be a pointer to the ever-recurring pattern of power politics manifesting in deceptions of deputations as is evident in the Peshwa-Phadnavis-Kotwal relationship. The bitter reality is this that as long as politics remains a power game, Nana Phadnavis, Ghasirams and Lalita Gauris are bound to emerge.

Acknowledged as a musical historical, *Ghasiram Kotwal,* owes its power and vibrancy to its delineation of contemporary socio-political reality. It also testifies to Tendulkar's stand as a creative writer as stated below:

> My creative writing, including the plays and films I have written, have mostly dealt or tried to deal with my contemporary social reality. As a social being, I am against all exploitation and I passionately feel that all exploitation must end.[3]

Ghasiram Kotwal, based on history, is not exactly a historical play. According to Tendulkar:

> Although based on historical legend, I have no intention of commenting on the morals, or lack of them, of the Peshwa, Nana Phadnavis or Ghasiram. The moral of this story, if there is any, may be looked for elsewhere.[4]

In reference to the relevance of the play in the Indian society today as it were in the Pune society in the eighteenth century, Tendulkar affirms that:

> In my view *Ghasiram Kotwal* indicates a particular situation, which is neither old nor new. It is beyond time and space. Therefore Ghasiram and Nana are also beyond space and time.[5]

The significance of the play does not lie in its depiction or distortion of the reality. To quote Tendulkar again:

> The play in not historical but is cooked in somewhat historical kitchens. It goes against the integrity of a creative piece of writing to be called historical or social. Time can quickly turn social into historical and historical into mythological. The story is not so important as what it signifies.[6]

The action of the play goes like this: On his first visit to Pune, Ghasiram, a Brahnmin from Kannauj, finds himself falsely accused of theft and slighted by the Pune Brahmins. He swears revenge on the city. He snares Nana Phadnavis, the Peshwa's chieftain and magistrate of the city using his young daughter Lalita Gauri. In return, Ghasiram demands to be appointed the Kotwal and is put in charge of the law and order of Pune. He now wastes no time in getting even with his former tormentors. But he does not realize that Nana is merely using him to keep the Brahmins in check; Ghasiram will become a convenient fall guy for Nana once he has accomplished his mentor's dirty job. As Ghasiram becomes the scourge of the city Brahmins, Nana savours Gauri's innocent charms. Then Ghasiram learns one day that Gauri had died mysteriously, and Nana is marrying for the seventh time. Insane with rage, the livid father confronts Nana, only to be reminded that his daughter's life was a small price to be paid for power and privilege. By this time, the city Brahmins have united in a bloodthirsty demand for Ghasiram's death. Nana signs the death warrant as casually as he had granted Ghasiram the Kotwali. The final scene shows Ghasiram being mobbed by the irate crowd he asks for death. As the crowd gathers round Ghasiram's lifeless body, Nana appears to herald the end of an age of terror and prospers festivities to mark the purging of the city and the play comes to an end.

*Ghasiram Katwal* is based on a historical incident. Balaji Janardhan Bhanu (1742-1800) was the Peshwa's Phadnavis of Pune. A shrewd statesman, he retained his power till his death. He kept the Maratha Empire free of British aggression by means of his astute political strategy and statesmanship. He was a cult hero whose flaws were ignored by the people. Being blind to their hero's treachery, they were only too ready to stone to death their kotwal when their Phadnavis asked them to do so. However, it was this respect of the Phadnavis' character that Tendulkar chose to highlight.

On responding to a query, regarding his choice of theme and form, by Samik Bandopadhyay, Tendulkar wrote:

> Ghasiram started with a theme, then came the specific 'story' or incident, which was historical and then, the search for the form began... By a series of accidents I discovered the present form which is a combination of a variety of ingredients from different folk forms of Maharashtra.[7]

Ghasiram, the protagonist, a poor Brahmin from Kannauj, comes to Pune in search of a livelihood. When we see him first, he has no high hopes for life. What worries him is how to earn a living for his family in the caste society of Pune. Thendulkar skillfully brings out the tragic element in Ghasiram by setting him against a mighty exploitative system, which attempts to strip him off his modesty and humanity. He finds himself misfit in Pune, which is dominated by the Brahmin folk. Ghasiram is denied entry into their society for he has a non-pious look, unshaven head and looks like a scoundrel. Ghasiram puts up with all sorts of humiliation in his quest for identity, and somehow shrewdly knows how to assert himself. He takes refuge in Bavannakhani where Gulabi, a courtesan, entertains Nana and his followers with dance and song. The Brahmins, like their ruler Nana, with a lack of morality, married seven times, still running after young women, are corrupt out and out. The decadence of the class in power is evoked brilliantly, when the sutradhar tells:

> Night comes
> Pune Brahmins go
> To Bavannakhani.... they go to the cemetery
> To the Kirtan... To the temple
> As they have done everyday.
> The night progresses... the Peshwa's Cheif Minister,
> Nana of the nine courts... of wealth and power
> Nana Phadnavis to Gulabi's palace proceeds.[8]

Thus both Nana and his subjects make most of their power and indulge in all kinds of indecent activities. Obsessed with unbridled sex, Nana neglects his duties. The Brahmins taking advantage of the situation, release terror in Pune. As a result, the innocent and helpless people like Ghasiram suffer for no fault of theirs. Unaware of their status, which is on top of social hierarchy, they come out to be lesser mortals. Being self-possessive they seek pleasure in the company of other women and fail to know what their women actually want. Ironically, the women are equally corrupt. They wish to enjoy themselves as much as their men do as is clear from their solicitation of the Maratha paramours in the absence of their spouses. It is this immorality on the part of men and women, which is typical of the modern society and stifles the springs of genuine human love. The Brahmins are unfaithful not only to their wives but also to their master, using religion as a cover to hide their misdeeds. The hypocrisy of the Brahmins is brought out in thin attribution of sacredness to their immoral acts. They regard Bavannakhani, the most sought after red light area, as "Mathura Avatarli" (GK 18) associated with Lord Krishna. This reflects the height of irreverence towards the religious institutions, which, built to uphold their right to superiority, are transformed into centres of exploitation of the needy. In fact, Tendulkar seems to suggest that 'the operation of religiosity, sexuality and deputationist politics serve as devices of power.'

Nana Phadnavis turns a blind eye to the corruption among his subjects. Like a modern politician, he knows how to make it to power. Thus he enjoys himself, while the people suffer. Ghasiram forced into this world of corruption, struggles to keep himself untainted. Having consciousness of his hazardous condition, he bears insult at the hands of the Puneites. The repeated humiliations shake the very foundations of his belief in human values.

The seeds of power are not sown in him till the middle of the play, but every effort he makes to keep his family up leads him to a realization that in a world where humanity is at a discount, it is hard to assert his individuality. So Ghasiram searches for a way out. He learns that it is Nana, the all powerful, who could help him out. Thus, he accepts to work for Gulabi only to meet Nana who visits her regularly.

He confronts him for the first time when the latter sprains his ankle while dancing with Gulabi. Ghasiram milks the situation, resting his injured leg on his back. Such resourcefulness of Ghasiram earns him both the favour of Nana and the wrath of the Brahmins. Seeing in him a threat to their existence, they make his life miserable and try to turn him out of their society. In reality, the Brahmins feel as insecure as Ghasiram. Tendulkar portrays excellently the pathetic condition of the Brahmins in a scene of Dakshina ceremony. Nana makes a mockery of this sacred ceremony by using it as a device to achieve his selfish ends. He feels happy as the Brahmins in their eagerness to grab the gifts, fight like dogs. When Ghasiram tries to join them for alms, they throw him out. They hand him over to the soldiers, blaming him for the theft of a purse. In spite of his innocence, he is punished severely. Ghasiram struggles to make his presence felt. But in a world where hatred, jealousy and immorality are the order of the day, even the most innocent people like Ghasiram are bound to be affected. Ghasiram's confrontation with the soldiers and his humiliation precipitate his innermost protest against injustice and inhumanity. Being motivated by a powerful vindictive desire, he swears to teach a lesson to the perpetrators of crime.

Ghasiram knows that Nana is a womanizer and can do anything for the sheer company of a woman. As such, he plans to please Nana by using his own daughter as bait to obtain a position in Nana's court. He angrily declares:

> I'll come back... to Pune; I'll show my strength. It will cost you! Your good days are gone... you've made me an animal. I'll be a devil inside. I'll make Pune a kingdom of pigs. (GK 26-27)

Ironically, it is this indiscriminate opportunism, which becomes the cause of Ghasiram's downfall.

Nana is much infatuated with the beauty of Ghasiram's daughter. He meets her at a religious ceremony, where he ogles at her. Ironically when the girl, chased by him, points to an idol, warning him "he will see", he explains mockingly: "the idol of holiness? The maker of good? Look, he has two wives, one on this side, and one on that side. If you sit on our lap, he won't say anything." (GK 28).

It is this disregard of the established institutions, which, although as a result of his insatiable desire for sex, symbolizes the decadent human values of the modern society. The idol, a substitute for an invisible god, is worshipped by human beings and is believed to generate awe and fear among the wrong doers and keeps men on the path of rectitude. But when man, out of selfishness, plays god himself, the cult of idol-worship loses all its significance and becomes a device in the hands of the vested interests to perpetuate exploitation.

As such, Nana being a slave to passions, has transformed Pune into a playground for the pleasure seekers. It is this life of immorality against which Ghasiram wages a war and becomes a martyr in the process. Seeing Nana's craving for Gauri, Ghasiram hands his daughter over to Nana with a sense of success in trapping Nana through sex. For a moment he is torn by a conflict between an individual motivated by a sense of revenge and a responsible father. He feels the prick of conscience and cries out: "Oh, my daughter...the beast. (Then vells at the audience) oh you people. Look! I've given my beloved daughter into the jaws of that wolf! Look. Look at this father...spit on me. Shove me." (GK 31) but Ghasiram is left with no other alternative than to sacrifice his daughter to realize his dream—dream of turning the city of Pune into a kingdom of pigs and of wielding unquestionable power. He exploits Nana's sexual weakness to his advantage. Thus we find in Ghasiram a metamorphosis from a docile father to a cunning schemer.

Knowing that Nana is obsessed with his daughter, Ghasiram like a clever politician, tries to make a deal with him:

> Sir, there's a way. People will not talk, my daughter will not be humiliated openly in Pune—if you make...me the Kotwal of Pune. (GK 33)

Ironically enough, Ghasiram, who wants to drive sin out of Pune, commits himself a terrible sin by prostituting his own daughter. Although, Ghasiram, prompted by a desire to chastise his tormenters, surrenders 'his heart's child' to Nana, the devil, for mere Kotwalship, he is fully aware of his sin and wishes to save Gauri once he is declared Kotwal of Pune.

However, what makes for his tragedy is his failure to understand the situation in which he moves. He cannot understand the designs of Nana and unwittingly gets into the trap laid by the latter. Ghasiram feels that he has succeeded in his clever plan, but tragically, he does not foresee the future trap into which he is entering. Nana has double advantage in appointing Ghasiram as the Kotwal: one, sexual, and two, political. He can enjoy his daughter as well as use him to control the Brahmins of Pune. Nana's words reveal his inner motive:

> Go Ghasya, old bastard. We made you Kotwal. Raise hell if you wish. But you don't know the ways of this Nana. This time, there are two bullets in this gun. With the first one we'll fell your daughter. But with the second one we'll make the city of Pune dance. Ghasya, child, you're a foreigner. I've put you on Pune's back. Why? As a countercheck to all those conspirators. You'll not be able to join them; they'll never trust you even if you do, because you are a stranger, an outsider. We just raised a dog at our door to the Kotwali. We are sole support. Oh! You're a bastard, Ghasya...our misdeeds will be credited to your account. We do; our Kotwal pays. This opportunity comes in the shape of Ghasiram. And that luscious peach is at hand to be bitten by Nana. Excellent! Yes Ghasya, be Kotwal. This Nana blesses you. (GK 34-35)

Ghasiram takes on the duty of looking after Pune. He does his work sincerely. He enforces the laws strictly and declares that the transgressors shall be punished severely. As a result there is an enormous fall in the crime rate. Scared by his method of punishment, the Brahmins shudder at the mention of his name. He announces that nothing can be done without his notice. Permits should be obtained "to kill a pig, to do an abortion, to be a pimp, to steal, to live with one's divorced wife, to remarry...to commit suicide." (GK 38).

Surprisingly, Ghasiram blinded by his success, turns demoniac. His imposition of rules on the behaviour of the people reaches the height of absurdity. He misuses his power. For a moment, the city of Pune seems to get rid of its vulgarity under the strict vigilance of Ghasiram Kotwal, but there is a rise in evil activities too. The effect of absolute power on Ghasiram makes him ruthless, sadist and high-handed in his treatment of the people who have hurt his feelings earlier. He employs savage techniques to elicit truth from culprits. No doubt, the Kotwalship serves as a means to bring about a change in the city but soon he becomes impatient and fails to understand the real causes for the crimes of the people. In no time, he becomes unpopular.

Ghasiram has been digging his grave inch-by-inch following the path of callousness and vindictiveness. The moral law, which he has been violating, will one day assert itself and crush him. His crimes border on sins and will be balanced by retribution. Being ignorant of all this, he continues with his work which adds to the dramatic irony. But then in the course of these things, though he appears to be carried away by absolute power, he is aware of his responsibility as a father. Like every father, he thinks, "it's easy to find a bride groom when one has money, jewels and respect." (GK 48) but he receives a blow when he hears of his daughter's death. Shocked, as he is, Ghasiram rushes to Nana to know why his daughter died. The political fox Nana somehow pacifies him through his words and offering of power. Ironically, though Ghasiram is still under Nana's spell he has changed for worse. The power with which he wanted to enhance the happiness of his daughter has made him impotent.

Such a shock transforms Ghasiram into a fiend who suddenly shuts his eyes to immorality and plunges headlong into a career of bloodshed. Unable to tolerate the hardships at cruel Ghasiram's hands, the Brahmins raise their voice against him and plead with Nana, who has been waiting for an opportunity and known "how to use a thorn to remove a thorn." (GK 63) and encourages them to finish Ghasiram. They play ends with Ghasiram being stoned to death.

Ghasiram in his quest for power confronts Nana, and plays his game to become the Kotwal of Pune foolishly thinking that the Kotwali will mean power in his hands, but Nana knows "what'll happen in that our misdeeds will be credited to your account." (GK 35). As such, Ghasiram is outwitted at the game of power played by Nana who exploits him as long as he needs him and drops him brutally in the end. Ghasiram's transformation from a poor and helpless Brahmin to a high-handed Kotwal is a journey from the world of innocence of the world of experience.

The title of the play, itself captivates its essence. It unites the public and the private being of a man. It is the transformation of a simple, unassuming man into a hubristic power crazy monster. The unsuspecting victim of a Machiavellian system embodied in the machinations of Nana, the true villain emerges unscathed from the turmoil that marked the rise and fall of Ghasiram.

The punishment meted out to Ghasiram proves the formula that who negates the universal order gets negated by it ultimately. It is this law of retribution, which is expressed in the words of Nana,

> 'Ladies and gentlemen! Citizens of Pune. A threat to the great city of Pune has been ended today (the crowd cheers). A disease has been controlled. The demon Ghasiram Kotwal, who plagued all of us, has met his death....everything has happened according to the wishes of the gods....' (GK 65-66).

Ghasiram rightly deserves our pity for the punishment greater than he deserved. There is a tragic sense of waste illustrated by the death of Ghasiram. Tendulkar has presented a very striking picture of a tragic figure like Ghasiram. The play, though inherently violent, never for once, deteriorates into a melodrama. There are in it scenes of torture and violence, but they do not manifest physically. It shown through physical gestures of the chorus and through the words of the sutradhar. The violence that we come across in the play testifies of Tendulkar's awareness of the violence in the psyche of modern man.

Ghasiram Savaldas belongs not only to the late eighteenth century Peshwa Empire, but also to all phases of human history. His rise and growth from a Savaldas to the most controversial Kotwal of Pune is symbolic of the multifaceted growth of corruption in our society. Through the shrewd and opportunistic character of Ghasiram, Tendulkar has tried to bring out the truth that sycophancy not only flourishes but also prospers under the patronage of the rulers.

Ghasiram knowingly puts his daughter at the disposal of a wolf-like Nana so as to satisfy his ambition. As a Kotwal he gets complete hold over the city of Pune and behaves with the people in a ruthless manner. He gives physical as well as mental torture to the common, innocent people. His cruelty crosses all the limits of reasonable human behaviour. Ghasiram is stoned to death on account of his indiscriminately revengeful spirit. He chooses evil deliberately, sticks to it and finally pays for it.

On looking at the play also from a feministic point if view, it presents a very moving, even shocking picture of the ruthless suppression of feminine consciousness. Tendulkar shows how vulnerable Indian women are in our patriarchal society. Ghasiram, the eponymous father, does not hesitate in bargaining the chastity of his daughter for his own selfish desire to avenge his humiliation on the people of Pune. For Nana Phadnavis, woman is an object of sexual gratification only. Nana procures Gauri by making Ghasiram the Kotwal of Pune and for sometime, as is reported by the sutradhar: "Ghasiram says, Nana does, Ghasiram's reign is here." (GK 36). Nana however has such an endless lust for women that he always needs a beautiful girl and a new bride for the gratification of his sexual urges. Gauri's physical charms cannot satisfy him for long and it is soon reported that Nana is marrying a girl of fourteen. Marriage is considered to be the holiest of holy institutions in our society. But Nana has a different way of looking at the sanctity of marriage. In spite of having several wives he's still going to marry a small girl. The sutradhar reports:

> Let's go to the wedding
> The Peshwa's Chief Minister
> Still young enough to marry!

He's got six wives
Look-that's not enough!
So he's got a new one. (GK 40)

Woman has no choice of her own in a male dominated society and the situation is the same whether she is Gulabi or Gauri or the newly wed wife of Nana or the old wives of Nana. Woman has always been a slave to her male counterpart, be it the eighteenth century or the twenty-first century.

The play is an ironical commentary on our socio-political set up. Tendulkar could find a parallel in the history of Peshwa Empire and thereby suggest that such circumstances are not confined to a particular era but are seen in all times and discovered its contemporary relevance. When we see the end of one Ghasiram, we presume that it is the end of all Ghasirams, but the fact is that the emergence of Ghasirams is a universal phenomenon. Ghasirams grow and prosper as and when they get identical socio-political situations in our society. In this context, Samik Bandopadhyay's observation is quite significant: "Nana needs Ghasiram, and Ghasiram needs Nana; but in the shifting game of power, it is only a temporary adjustment that Nana exploits as long as necessary and can drop unceremoniously the moment it has served its purpose."[9]

Religion, sex and deputationist politics operate as different but complimentary devices of power in our society and Tendulkar has presented it very well in the play. In depicting the rise and growth of Ghasiram in our society, Tendulkar seems to have suggested that the purpose of the drama is not to produce catharsis i.e. 'peace of mind, all passion spent', but to encourage, stimulate and provoke the audience/reader to think over the issues affecting the normal and balanced growth of human society. By showing the fatal end of Ghasiram in the play, Tendulkar does not want to suggest the Ghasiram has ended forever. He rather wants to draw our attention to the socio-political factors responsible for the growth of such a crisis in our society. There are certain questions that keep haunting our minds: what led to the emergence of Ghasiram? Who is responsible for the rise and growth of Ghasiram? And what are the fatal consequences arising out of the creation of

Ghasiram? The contemporary relevance of the play lies in the answer to these questions, and here Tendulkar stands firmly as a class in himself.

In Shanta Gokhale's words: "Ghasiram Kotwal is a political comment about the creation, by political parties in power, of monsters for temporary gain, leading to iniquity, brutality and ultimate destruction",[10] and Tendulkar himself has agreed that the play is primarily "a study of the power game."[11] His choice of subject itself indicates this. In words of Gayle Greene and Coppelia Kahn:

> Women are the gifts which men exchange between each other...they are gifts, not givers. They have no significant power or influence within a system, which is controlled by men and works to their benefit. Men, not women, have the power to determine the values of women in the exchange and the meanings associated with them.[12]

Tendulkar throughout the play has used female sexuality to represent the loss and destruction caused by the struggle for power. The corruption that power brings about is projected through the sexual laxity of the Brahmin dominated society of Pune. The play was attacked by those who perceived the play as an attack on the character of Nana Phadnavis, the finest administator and one of the greatest patriots of the Maratha Empire. Tendulkar responded to this criticism by pointing out that Ghasiram Kotwal was not meant to be a historically accurate account of Nana or Ghasiram's character or the rule over Pune. The most important thing is that he has examined the very modern issue of the relationship between power and gender in a patriarchal society in a historical setting with historically recognizable characters. By locating the story in the past and by associating it with a much admired and revered national figure, Tendulkar has underlined both the dark ambiguity of the cardboard figures of power which the male dominated society holds in high esteem and the dangers of this struggle for power in which gender has always played an important part. Meaning of gender in patriarchy is not just "difference" but "division, oppression, inequity and inferiority for women"[13] and thus for all those without access to power.

Tendulkar in Ghasiram Kotwal suggests that the social construction of gender is effectively a useful tool in the hands of the powerful and will lead inevitably to the dehumanizing of both the powerful and the powerless alike, the Nanas and the Ghasirams as much as the Gauris, and also to the destruction of meaningful human relationships and social and moral values.

While unfolding the plot of the play we come across an explosive picture of the moral decadence of the Pune Brahmins during the decline of the Peshwa regime, painted by Tendulkar. With unique imagination and invention he has created his own theatrical reality by using a variety of functionally effective theatre forms such as mime, drama, music and dialogue in verse. "He has blended this mixture with an aritstic touch which is incomparable in the annals of Marathi theatre."[14]

The popularity of the play can be seen in the controversy it created recently when it was staged abroad. Balachandra Kelkar, the Founder President of the P.D.A. said while banning the play: "...patriotic Maratha chancellor Nana Phadnavis has been portrayed as lecherous character and a golden period of the Peshwa rule has been shown as a period of decadence."[15]

Countering the charges, Tendulkar said that Ghasiram Kotwal was not a historical play and he had merely used some historical anecdotes and incidents to project the contemporary caste politics and power game in which women have been used. He explained: "History interests me only in so far as it relates to my period and the situation around me."[16]

Thus Ghasiram Kotwal is an attack on the moral downfall of the ruling class of Maharashtra who considered themselves custodians of public morality. It comments acerbically on political institutions of present day India where scores of Ghasirams are made and marred each time the political die is cast anew. The impulse to write the play was provoked by the contemporary political situation of the time, specifically the rise of power of the Shiv Sena in Maharashtra.

## NOTES

1. Samik Bandopadhyay, 1999. "Introduction: *Ghasiram Kotwal* by Vijay Tendulkar. Kolkata: Seagull Books.
2. Ibid.
3. Ibid.
4. "Introduction", p. iv.
5. *Ghasiram Kotwal*, 1983. Hindi trans. Vasant Deo. New Delhi: Radhakrishan.
6. Ibid.
7. "Introduction", 3.
8. Vijay Tendulkar, 1999. *Ghasiram Kotwal*. Calcutta: Seagull Books. 16-17. The subsequent references from this play will be cited from this edition.
9. "Introduction", 3.
10. Shanta Gokhale, 1999. "On Ghasiram Kotwal", in Vijay Tendulkar's *Ghasiram Kotwal*, trans. Jayant Karve and Eleanor Zelliot. Calcutta: Seagull Books. 81-82.
11. Samik Bandopadhyay, "Introduction".
12. Gayle Greene and Coppelia Kahn, 1985. "Feminist Scholarship and Social Construction of Woman", *Making a Difference: Feminist Literary Criticism*. London: Methuen, 7.
13. Ibid., 4.
14. Dhyaneshwar Nadkarni, Jan.-Feb. 1973. "Tendulkar's Ghasiram Kotwal", Enact, no. 73-74 (Jan-Feb 1973).
15. M.L. Kulkarni, 1973. "Ghasiram Kotwal", NCPA. 11, 3.
16. *The Indian Express*, August 24, 1986. "*Ghasiram Kotwal*—Fact or Fiction."

# Myth, History and Tradition: A Study of Girish Karnad's *Hayavadana* and *Tughlaq*

8

*Jayadeep Sarangi*

Girish Karnad, a recipient of the Jnanpith Award, an actor, a film producer, is regarded as a very significant playwright of the post-Independent Indian literature, Karnad's whole corpus can be divided into two broad based categories: Myth-plays and history-plays. In *Naga-Mandala, Yayati, Hayavadana* and *The Fire and the Rain* we find the predominance of mythical element. In *Tale - Danda* and *Tughlaq*, we find a predominant historical structure. Girish Karnad treats "history as myth and rather that writing a strictly factual historical play he gives it symbolical reshaping to reinforce the contemporary issues." (Dixit 2003: 86)

Girish Karnad's *Hayavadana* (1975), a play in two acts, is his third play. Originally written in Kannada, the play was an immediate success on the stage and received the prestigious Kamala Devi Chhattopadhyaya award of 1971. The playwright himself translated it into English retaining, however, the original title, *Hayavadana*. 'Hayavadana' literally means 'one with a horse's head'. The precursor text is The Transposed Heads by Thomas Mann. *Hayavadana* has one main plot and one subplot. The story of *Hayavadana* constitutes the sub-plot while the main plot is based on the story of 'The Transposed Heads' in the Sanskrit *Vetala-Panchavimsati* which forms the part of a large *Kathasaritsarara* of Somadeva of the 11th Century. There are twenty-five stories of King Vikrama and Vetala in it. each of these stories poses a riddle at the end, which Vetala challenges the King to solve. While the Indian solution in *Vetalapanchavimsati* upholds idealism, the German solution is "The Transposed Heads" champions materialism. Aware of the extreme nature of these opinions, Karnad seems to hint at "the middle course of humanism in Hayavadana." (Dhanavel 2000: 37).

In *Hayavadana*, we find the mythical story of a Gandharva and the shape-shifting to a stallion (fully grown male horse that has to be castrated, especially one used for breeding) due to a curse. Shape-shifting is a typical device employed by Karnad in his plays. Shape-shifting has been defined as change of forms by the cultural anthropologists. Indian myths and legends have plenty of instances of shape-shifting: plant changing to an animal, man changing to an animal; women become a bird; and a dead person becomes alive. In *Naga-Mandala*, the Naga assumes a human shape off and on; in fact, he disguises himself in the shape of Rani's husband. In *Hayavadana* Kapila and Devdatta behead themselves, and when granted the boon by Goddess Kali, Padmini joins their heads on each other's body. The result is chaotic. Not only the main plot, but also the sub-plot is related to head shifting (a part of shape-shifting) of Hayavadana, a creature with human body and the head of a horse. In *Hayavadana*, the heads of Kapila and Devadatta are exchanged. Hayavadana puts forward his case of incompleteness very impressively. Hayavadana's image brings the Lacanian[1] subject – incomplete, incoherent, fragmented, divided and centreless. The image of Ganesha works as the prototype of the main symbol – a man's body with an elephant's head and a broken tusk. The god is not complete by Mysteriously he is the "destroyer of incompleteness." The dramatized image of Ganesha projects the Lacanian subject. The protagonists of the sub-plot, Hayavadana, has a human body and equine head but is not a God like Ganesha. Thought he is born of a gandharva father, he is not one because he does not have divine power like his father to change his own shape or that of other. Karnad uses the folk form and assimilates into it the tradition of Indian classical drama, the Western dramatic conventions to convey his perception of contemporary reality. *Hayavadana* opens with the offering classical tradition, wherein the beginning of a drama some god or goddess is invoked for blessing. In 'Yakshagana', it is Lord Ganesha, the god of success that is invoked. At the beginning of the performance, a mask of

Ganesha is brought on the stage and kept on the chair. In the pooja and prayer, Lord Ganesha is addressed as 'single tusked destroyer of incompleteness.' (p. 73). Here, the choice of the elephant – headed god is significant because Lord Ganesha with human body and animal head properly suggests the central theme of incompleteness of being. Lord Ganesha is worshipped as the destroyer of incompleteness. Bhagavata rightly comments: "An elephant body, a broken tusk and cracked belly – whichever way look at it seems to be an embodiment of imperfection of incompleteness" (73). By involving the Lord Ganesha and its myth Karnad reconciles the tradition and modernity into an organic synthesis. We are aware of the myth of Ganesha's origin. One of fescinating aspects of dealing with myths is their self-reflexivity. A myth is complete in itself when examined in detail, contains "subconscious signals which lead you to another myth which in turn act as a conduit to a third one while illuminating the one you started with" (Karnad 1998: 69). Girish Karnad is no stranger to the "World of Indian myths, including the epics and Puranas." (Dhanavel 2000: 57) As his contemporary playwright Vijay Tendulkar rightly on serves, Karnad was "groomed in mythology" (Ramnarayan 1989: 15) Karnad has admitted on more than one occasion that he grew up with "a lot of myths" (Chakraborty 1991: 48).

The other important device drawn from the Indian regional folk theatre tradition is the use of half-curtain. Half-curtain is used throughout the play as a very important stage property. Karnad believes in the presentation of the on stage. He gives full freedom to the directors of his plays. Half-curtain is effective in the presentation of *Hayavadana*. By bringing down the curtain the horse is exposed and concealed a few times. With a device of a curtain depicting a blazing fire, the impression is given on the stage that Padmini is consumed by the fire. Behind the curtain the terrifying of goddess Kali with the blood-red uplifted palms and mouth open with tongue lolling out is shown. While using the folk strategy of half-curtain, Karnad modernizes it by giving it a symbolic significance. While dealing with complex states of minds, the half-curtain comes in very handy. 'Yakshagana' is a special feature of the folk dance drama of coastal Karnataka. Karnad uses mask in the play which is the characteristic feature of Indian folk theatre. The first mask is that of Ganesha, the destroyer of obstacles. Later Devadatta in opening of the play appears on the stage wearing a palecoloured mask and Kapila a dark mask. Later in the play, masks are transposed to indicate the transposition of heads. Kali, the goddess, appears in a terrible mask and Hayavadana appears at first wearing the mask of a horse's head and later when he becomes a complete horse he wears the mask of a complete horse. In the process, 'part' becomes the 'whole'; organs become the complete body. *Hayavadana* is play of growth a chronological maturity to a 'full' shape of organs (comdined into a body). Lord Ganesha is physically incomplete and yet he is the destroyer of incompleteness.

The imagery of the play is specifically Indian. Devadatta characterizes Padmini as "Shyama Nayika – born of Kalidasa's magic description as Vatsyayana had dreamt her" (p. 14). Padmini describes the coming of the dawn in the forest: "The shadows of twigs draw alpanas on the floor. The stars raise arati and go" (p. 52). Padmini's situation is beautifully summed up by the images of the river and the scare crows in the choric songs. When Padmini observes a sati, the females declared, "Our sister is leaving in a palanquin of sandalwood. Her mattress is studded with rubies which burn and glow. She is decked in flowers which blossom on tinder-wood and whose petals are made of molten gold. How the garlands leap and cover her a flame with love" (p. 47). This imagery is suggestive. Instances of Indian Idiom are, 'One has to collect merit in seven lives to get a friend like him' (p. 21) and Padmini's description of her husband as "you are my saffron, my marriage thread, my deity" (p. 21).

Bhagavata, who introduces the story, is the stage manager of the classical Sanskrit drama. By using Bhagavata and the kind of role which Karnad assigns to the Bhagavata outgrows the traditional role. However, in keeping with the folk tradition he narrates the story in the manner of a folk tale: "Our duty is merely to pay homage to the elephant – heated god and get on with the play" (p. 73) and he begins: "This is the city of Bharmpura, ruled by King Dharmasheela whose fame and empire have already reached the ends of the eight direction ...." (p. 73). Bhagavata takes charge of the play's opening when the Nata frightened by a speaking Hayavadana, creates a disturbance on the stage. He also decides the time when the half-curtain must be brought in or withdrawn. He initiates the discussion and invites responses to the actions of the characters. He is involved intimately with every character. He expresses sympathy for Kapila when he is forsaken by Devadatta and Padmini after the transposition. When Padmini transposes the heads there is a problem of identity. Bhagavata solves this problem by the rishi's verdict. He suggests Hayavadana to go to the temple of Kali at Chitrakoot. Thus, the role of Bhagavata is of a helper, a part-narrator, commentator and an interpreter of the events. The play opens with Bhagavata's prayer of Lord Ganesha and ends with his praise of Lord Ganesha. He says that the mercy of the Elephant-headed Ganesha is unfathomable. Bhagavata plays the role of the Breachtian narrator.

In the classical drama, the chorus plays an important role. They sang and dance on the stage. In *Hayavadana*, the chorus plays a subordinate role to Bhagavata. Bhagavata is the head of the musicians, stage manager and the interpreter. The play begins with a prayer to Lord Ganesha. In Act II, we listen to the female chorus. Bhagavata throws light on Padmini's predicament by giving an example of a river and a scare crow. The female chorus then sings:

The river only fells the pulls of the waterfall.
She giggles and tickles the rushes
On the banks, then turns ..... (p. 57)

When Padmini performs Sati, the female chorus sings a dirge. Here, the chorus ironically celebrates Padmini's desire and voluntary death. The women declare: "Our sister is leaving in a palanquin of sandalwood. Her mattress is studded with rubies which burn and glow. She is decked in flowers which blossom on tinder-wood and whose petals are made of molten gold. How the garlands leap and cover her aflame with love." (p. 65)

In the last song of the female chorus, the women ask the question, "Why should love stick to the sap of a single body? When the stem is drunk with the thick yearning of the many petalled, many-flowered lantana why should it be tied down to the relation of a single flower ?" (p. 70). Here, Karnad has introduced the chorus with a definite purpose. He uses the female chorus just like T.S. Eliot's *Murder in the Cathedral* but he puts it in a different sense.

*Tughlaq*, a historical play, was originally written in Kannada in 1964 and Girish Karnad was persuaded to translate it into English by Alyque Padamsee. This translation was first staged at the Bhulabhai Auditorium, Bombay, in August 1970. *Tughlaq* explores the ambiguous stand of the idealist Sultan Muhammad Tughlaq whose reign is known as one of the spectacular regimes of history. Girish Karnad (1999) himself writes:

> My subject was the life of Muhammad Tughlaq, a fourteenth century Sultan of Delhi, certainly the most brilliant individual ever to ascend the throne of Delhi and also one of the biggest failures. After a reign distinguished for policies that today seem far-sighted to the point of genius, but which in their day earned him the title, 'Muhammad the Mad', the Sultan ended his career in bloodshed and political chaos. In a sense, the play reflected the slow disillusionment my generation felt with the new politics of independent India: the gradual erosion of the ethical norms that had guided the movement for independence, and the coming to terms with cynicism and real politik. (Murthy 1972: viii).

Muhammad-bin-Tughlaq, the well-known king in Indian history, is known for his eccentricity, hypocrisy and insane policies than for anything else. The play offers a psycho-political study of the protagonist of the play – his historicity, motives, vision and struggle to assert himself as the Sultan, as also how he takes his own downfall.

Now let us examine the character of Tughlaq from the historical frame of references. After Ghiyas-ud-din Tughlaq's death in February or March, 1325, Ulugh Khan sat upon the throne under the title of Muhammad Tughlaq. For forty days he remained at Tughlaqabad, after which marched to the state-city of Delhi and took his seat on the throne in the Red Palace of Balban:

> The capital city was well decorated for his reception. The king threw gold and silver coins among the populace. His accession was well received by the people and there was no resolution and no opposition. People seem to have expected great things from him and he, too, seems to have been confident of doing better than the previous Sultans of Delhi. (Srivastava 1998: 207).

After his accession he issued many ordinances for the improvement of the administration and revenue. His next step was to increase taxation in the Doab with a view to augment his resources. Apart from the tax reform, he created a department of agriculture, which was called Diwan-I-Kohi. The main objective of this agricultural department was to bring the uncultivated land under cultivation by going direct monetary assistance from the state treasury. A controversial important political experiment of Muhammad Tughlaq was the transfer of the capital from Delhi to Devagiri which was renamed Daulatabad:

> ... Several reasons led to this fateful decision. The first was that Sultan was anxious to have a capital, which should not only be situated at a strategic place but should also be, in the center of his far-flung kingdom. Muhammad was impressed by Devagiri, and we are told by Barani that geographical importance of the place was one of the reasons for its selection as the metropolis. As he writes: "This held a central situation; Delhi, Gujarat Lakhanauti Satgaon, Sonargaon, Telang, Malabar, Dwarasamudra and Kampil were about equidistant from thence ..." Secondly, Delhi was too near the north-western frontier which was constantly threatened by Mongol raids, while the Sultan wanted the new capital to be at a safe distance from the invaders from the north-west. Thirdly, while northern

> India had almost been conquered and pacified, the Dakhin was a new and uneasy partner in Sultanate. It could be effectively subdued and managed by a government that had its headquarters in Southern India. Lastly, he must surely have felt that Southern India was so rich and that he would be able to utilize its resources more easily and effectively by an intimate contact with it. (Srivastava 1998: 211).

Muhammad ordered the people of Delhi to move to Daulatabad with all their belongings. Ibn Battuta tells us that he caused a search to be made and a blind man and a cripple were found in the city unwilling to leave. "It is said that the cripple was put to death, while the blind man was ordered to be dragged to Daulatabad with result only one of his legs reached the new capital." (Srivastava 1998: 210).

The entire scheme did not give any fruitful result. The Sultan did not realize that people would not abandon their shelters except in unavoidable circumstances like natural calamities. The Muslim population of Delhi was against the ideal that they had to live in the Hindu surroundings in the Dakhin. Muhammad Tughlaq is also known for his introduction of Token Currency. He has been called 'a prince of moneyers'. Like Balban, Muhammad believed that the Sultan is the "Shadow of God". Coins of his time bore the inscription "Al Sultan Zilli Allah" (Sultan, the Shadow of God).

No ruler in our medieval history has aroused so much interest and controversy that of Muhammad-bin-Tughlaq. He inherited a vast kingdom, which embraced not only the entire northern India but also the 'Dakhin'. But, his achievements were negative. Therefore, when he died, the Sultanate of Delhi was reduced in size. The 'Dakhin' was almost lost. Sindh was almost slipping away from his hand when he closed his eyes in death. Some of the modern historians opine that Muhammad has not responsible for his failure as a ruler he failed because circumstances were not in his favour. His failure was due to his characteristic limitations and to some odd decisions. Probably, he lacked practical knowledge and common sense.

In the final scene in spite of his secular outlook, generosity, personal ability, Muhammad was getting more and more unpopular. Elphinstone was the first historian who believed that Muhammad was a victim of insanity. Ibn Battuta definitely asserts that he was very meticulous in his daily prayers and other religions rites enjoyed by Islam. On the other hand, Barani says that the Sultan had lost faith in Islam and acted against its tenets. Therefore, we have contradictory frames of references regarding the historical facts of Tughlaq (Srivastava, 1998).

Why did this able emperor Muhammad Tughlaq fail and suffer? Patanjali, the ancient sage and psychologist of our country has traced the cause of man's failure and suffering to *klesas*. 'Abhinivesa' has been diagnosed as the cause of Muhammad's fall and suffering. 'Abhinivesa' is defined by Maharshi Patanjali as "Svarsa-vahi-viduso pi tatha rudhobhinivesah" (*The Bhagwad Gita* II: 9) 'Abhi' means in the direction of; 'ni' means downward; and 'vesa' means to enter. A man, even a wise man, has an innate interest/passion/notion. Gradually, this passion or notion enters deep down into the person and gets settled there. If a person acquires control (that of the good 'rider'), i.e. passion through some well directed guidance, then there isn't any tragedy, and if not then there is fall and suffering. The Sultan is the victin of 'abhinivesa', i.e., a deep-seated passion. We see no chances for his passion to be checked, reviewed and reshaped. The futility of his decisions is perceived by the alert people of his state. But the Sultan being possessed by stubborn 'abhinivesa' stands destined: fall and suffering on all fronts.

## NOTE

1. Jacques Lacan is one of the tripple pillars of the influential post-structuralist movement, the other two being Jacques Derrida and Michael Foucault.

## REFERENCES

Chakraborti, M. (1991). "Mousumi Chakraborti talks to Girish Karnad" Tenor 7 Sept. 46-50.

Dhanavel, P. (2000). *The Indian Imagination of Girish Karnad*. New Delhi: Prestige, 37, 57.

Dixit, S. (2003). *Myths in Girish Karnad's Plays: Studies in Indian Drama in English*, ed. A.N. Prasad et al. Bareilly: Prakash Book Depot, 86.

Karnad, Girish (1975). *Hayavadana*, Calcutta: OUP (All subsequent references are from this edition).

Karnad, Girish (1989). *Tughlaq*, Delhi: OUP (All subsequent references are from this edition).

Karnad, Girish (1998). *The Fire and the Rain*, Delhi: OUP, 09.

Murthy, U.R. (1972). "Introduction", *Tughlaq*, Delhi: OUP.

Ramnarayan, G. (1989). "A New Myth of Sisyphus" *Theatre: The Hindus Folio* (February, 8) 15.

*The Bhagwad Gita*. Gorakpur: Geeta Press, 1993, II: 9.

# Myth as Aesthetic Experience in Girish Karnad's *The Fire and The Rain*

9

*Ranjana Chanana*

Girish Karnad, a Padma Bhushan, won India's highest literacy prize Bhartiya Jnanpith in 1999. He has unique command over his dramatic material. He creates a new colour, new canvas, new sketches, almost a new environment by creating clash between ritual, reality and drama. The operation of Myth in *The Fire and The Rain* is developed in such a way as it brings forth the principles of dramaturgy and the motifs of drama that hold a mirror to the very evolution of a turly 'Indian Theatre which can be true to its traditions and at the same time responsive to contemporary concerns.' (*Hindu*)

*The Fire and The Rain* transcends barriers of language and constraints of a given culture to blossom into a drama with universal appeal (*The Indian Express*). Karnad searched and researched the contemporary realities for creating the aesthetic experience through drama—the ancient medium of art. He came across the story of Yavakri and Paravasu while still in college, in C. Rajagopalachari's abridgement of *Mahabharat*. The myth of Yavakri (or Yavakrita) was selected by Karnad from the Vanaprava of *Mahabharat* to give a Natya Rupa of 'Agni Mattu Male' in Kannada which he translated in English in 1998. Dramatic genius of Karnad explored through the ancient myth:

> I first came across the story of Yavakri and Paravasu, while still in college, in C. Rajagopalachari's confronted with the stupendous task of abridging the world's largest epic to about four hundred pages, should not have discarded this seemingly peripheral tale is a tribute to his sensitivity and judgement. It was fortunate for me that Rajaji did not do so, for the moment I read the tale, I knew it had to be

turned into a play. For the next thirty seven years, I struggled with it, trying to fit all the ramifications of the myth within some sort of a manageable shape."[1]

Karnad has worked out Yavakri myth with extensive and intensive motifs for showing the orbs and curves of human psyche. India is a land of myths. Mythical stories were described in Puranas to create awareness among common man so that they may understand the subtlety of Vedas. In order to educate men and women, to implement just practices and propound certain religious doctrines, myths and stories were created. That is why the teekakar of *Vishnu Puran* and *Vayu Puran* comments, "If certain things are exaggerated and unauthentic accounts are being narrated it is acceptable because the sole purpose of Puranas is to cultivate high standards in society so that it may function smoothly." Myths generally deal with the permanent and great problems in human life particularly in the field of love, war, sin, tyranny, courage, fate, hatred, and ambition. For Indians, there is no difference between life and literature, heart and mind, religion and culture. Karnad is deeply rooted in Indian culture and religion and his dramatic genius equipped with creative imagination explores the treaded and untreaded floors of human psyche:

> *Agni Mattu Male* (*The Fire and The Rain*) as the title itself suggests, is about the confrontation and fusion of opposites—in nature, art and society. At the heart of the play are Brahmanical fire rituals (a Yajna undertaken to please rain-god) and its non-Brahmanical parallel Natya or theatre. Paravasu who performs the sacred Yajna is guilty of patricide and untruth. He joins the rest in accusing his innocent brother, Arvasu of the crime (the younger brother who becomes an actor later, performs the Natya). The father, Raibhya, supposed to be a great sage is no better than a demon. He has destroyed his brother, is jealous of his son and sexually exploits his own daughter in law, Vishakha.[2]

To achieve the highest aesthetic experience of literature, one should see the fundamental aspect of "Rasa' which is based on conditioned responses. But it is something higher in itself. It may be called unconditioned or cultivated response. Bharatmuni gives the best analogy:

> Yatha hi na, na, vyanojanaus' adhi saniyogad rasanis' pattih tatha, na, na, bha, vopagama, d rasanis' patth.[3]

The unique taste of delicacy is achieved from coming together of many ingredients each of which has a particular taste like conditioned responses – sour, salty, sweet (according to analogy with cooking, which combines heat and expertise) but the taste of dish is different and is of a higher order rather unconditioned. *Dhvani* theorists Anandvardhana and Abhinavgupta focused on the roles played by *vacya* (connotative meaning) and *vacaka* (denotative meaning) for *bharkatva* or *vyanjakatava* (suggestive meaning) for the highest aesthetic experience in literature. *Dhvani* finally arises from the analytical procedure of Dhvanyaloka:

> Kavyasyatma sa evarthas tatha cadikaveh pura/
> Krauncadvandvaviyogottha sokah slokatvamagatah/[4]

K. Krishnamoorthy comments on the Dhvani theory that "Dhvani is the quintessence of poetry, and rasa is the quintessence of dhvani." Thus *dhvani* is the essence of poetry and *rasa* is its soul. *Alankara* and *vakrokti* also can not serve independently. They account for something higher, something major in poetry. Thus *alankar*, style, imagery and fable all contribute to 'rasanubhuti'. (Experience of Literary Flavours). Myth as the centripetal force of the unconscious mind emerging from the many sided force becomes the properties of *kavya pratibha* (poetic imagination) to a creative writer. Myth operates more powerfully and evocatively than the power of language itself. It spells bound the reader with mystifying effects and many new options of ideas. Myth affects more powerfully through suggestive language:

> The meaning of poetic words may be ambiguous or oblique but it is not wayward like the meaning of mythical images. Again, even at the risk of appearing simplistic, we might say that in poetry there is perfect concord between work and its meaning. A word used in myth have several

> meanings and all the meanings may be relevant and this cluster of meanings build in the fabric of the myth.[5]

To Anandvardhana, the real meaning of the words lies in its suggestive form. The myth of Yavakri remains an integral part of Karnad's psyche and forms its base for the artistic form of drama. Yavakri myth in *The Fire and The Rain* suggests more meanings which are above the connotative and denotative meanings. It mirrors the deeper structure of human behaviour and leaves the psychological effects of the myth on the social consciousness of human beings. Thus 'sanaketitartha' (universal acceptance of the meaning) – concept of *rasa* in association with *dhvani* is the process of creation, recreation and appreciation in achieving aesthetic experience. There is no *rasa* outside *natya*. If there is *rasa* in *kavya*, then it arises only when *kavya* is dramatized.

'Kavye' pi natyamaneva rasah.'[6] The role of different *bhavas* (emotions) such as *vibhavas* (universalized stimuli) *anubhavas* (universalized responses) and *vyabhicaribhavas* (universal moods and feelings in the form of sorrow, fear, disgust, love) in association formulate aesthetic experience but it is syntactic peculiarities, imagery reference, denotation and connotation in combination with *dhvani* itself that the *vyangyartha* (the suggested meaning) is realized by *sahrdaya* or responsive reader for *rasaswadan* (for the taste of *rasa*). A man of ordinary sight and understanding cannot experience *rasa*, it is only a creative writer, with deep thought and high soaring imagination, who transpersonalises human emotions which can be termed as 'sadharnikarana' which again can be understood as the objective representation of human emotions:

> 'Sadharnikarana' means universailization and transpersonalization. The peak of *rasa* realization is attained when the spectator's ties with their ego are snapped and they find themselves lifted from the plane of their sordid private lives to the plane of collective human existence.[7]

We may recall here Longinus' theory of Sublime which transports a reader out of himself. Longinus measures sublime move by its spirit than its form. Sublime always excites, moves, transports and elevates. Aristotle's theory of catharsis and *sadharnikarana* are identical as both the theories advance towards the level of ecstacy which makes the reader forget everything and reach the state of objectivity it enables her/him to experience aesthetic joy. Myth plays a great role as a religious and cultural force of society. It widens the artistic and imaginative range of the writer and the reader through symobls and suggestive images.

*The Fire and The Rain* presents the myth of *Mahabharat* symbolically and psychologically. Karnad has already proved his dramatic excellence while dealing with myths and symbols in *Yayati, Hayavadana, Naga Mandala* and *Tughlaq*. Whether it may be a traditional folk tale or historical tale, he as an expert psychologist explores the deeper regions of human brain. The play presents complicated human relationships and contrastive features (opposite elements). Yavakreeta myth centres round jealousy, revenge, curse in *Mahabharata* but Karnad has picked up the episode to relate to the modern context. He works on the myth for revealing the psychic aberrations. The jealousy of man against man can be seen in Yavakri – the son of sage Bharadwaj who burns incessantly through the fire of jealousy inside his body and mind. The jealousy that Yavakri nourishes in him against Raibhya and his sons symbolizes his unconscious mind. Karnad like a learned expert emphasizes the role of unconscious process of human behaviour. Freud in his book "The Ego and the Id" says:

> ........almost the entire mental life is directed from the unconscious forces. The conscious level is a very small part of the unconscious mind. The unconscious is the reservoir of the unfulfilled motives. It stores the repressed unfulfilled sexual desires. The repressed desires do not disappear but go to the unconscious of the man and there await suitable chances of manifestation.[8]

Yavakri feels humiliated as his father Bharadwaj, though a Brahmarshi, never thought of having social recognitions for his *Brahma Vidya* (divine knowledge). On the contrary Raibhya's two sons Paravasu and Arvasu were learned as they have mastered the mystical knowledge of Vedas by the grace of guru. The social prestige and priestly honours heaped on learned Raibhya and his son kindles fire in the heart of Yavakri and the flames reach his soul to the extent that he takes a vow to please God Indra for mastering all the sacred knowledge of the Vedas without the grace of any guru. Indra is pleased; he grants him his long, long cherished boon. He was a strong and determined person. Gifted with knowledge, he comes back to inform his father of his achievements. Bharadwaj is suspicious. So he wants his son not to challenge the real saint Raibhya. But Yavakri's egoism fails to control the self and he violates all the limits and corners Vishakha, the daughter-in-law of Raibhya. Yavakri's dialogue with Vishakha enables us to peep into the deep human psyche:

> The day I decided my penance was over I fell down in a dead faint. I don't know how long I was in that state. It was terrible exhaustion, the pain of sheer relief, and when I opened my eyes, do you know the first thing that I thought of? Ten years ago I had come to your house to bid you good-bye. And you led me quickly to the jackfruit grove behind your house. You opened the knot of your blouse, pressed my face to your breasts, then turned and fled. I stood there stunned. The trees were loaded with fruit. Many were ripe and split open and the rich golden segments poured out. The sweet sick smell of the jackfruit, the maddening hum of a fly. The smell of our body. Ten years later I opened my eyes and I knew I was hungry for that moment. (14)

Most of the human activities are motivated from the unconscious mind which includes those experiences which were because of their being painful or contrary to the social norms. Along with these, the unconscious consists of instinctive desires, which were not allowed to be expressed on the conscious level. These tendencies are mostly sexual while few are concerned with the ego as well. According to Adler, most of the unconscious tendencies are concerned with the desire of power. Yavakri's above statement is suggestive of his longing for that moment which he has been cherishing in his heart for ten years. Karnad's exhibition for a willing submission of Vishakha to the incestuous behest of Yavakri and derailing from the original episode of molestation of Raibhya's daughter in law shows some psychic aberrations and latent impulses for the fulfillment of repressed desires. Vishakha's response to Yavakri reveals about their deep repressed frustration and amazement at Yavakri's search for knowledge and his deep concentration and a steel hook of longing which could not be affected by time and weather:

> Vishakha: I can't believe it. The whole world may be singing your praises. But you haven't grown up! These ten years have not made any difference to your teenage fantasies. That's all gone, Yavakri. Indra may be immortal. But................my breasts hang loose now. (Laughs)
>
> Yavakri: Why are you laughing?
>
> Vishakha: I have been trembling at the sight of you these last three days. Now, I only feel sorry.
>
> Yavakri: Good. I told you, you could go home if you were angry. But you are not angry. My tale only makes you feel sorry for me. So you can stay?
>
> Vishakha: The moment I heard you say you were hungry for words, I knew it was too late to go. I coudn't walk out on you after that. I had lost the initiative—missed the moment of decision. Because I know that hunger well, Yavakri. That's why I should have gone back without saying a word to you. (14-15)

Vishkha tells Paravasu about her making love to Yavakri before her father in law Raibhya would complain to his sons. She tells:

> At least Yavakri was warm, gentle, for a few minutes, he made me forget the wizard body, the scratchy claws and the blood cold as ice. And he paid it for his life. (33)

Lacan—the post-structural critic finds a close connection between the text and the language used by the individual. Lacan's criticism throws light on the unconscious mind of a human being. Words are not limited to what is said, they express more than the words themselves. The split of emotions and the ambivalence bring the negative chain of human ideas creating tension in the inner regions of Vishakha's psyche. The complexities arising out of the process of repression and depression due to isolation and alienation fills Vishakha with *dainya bhava*—depressive mood. This mood of fearfulness about her proving a whore by Raibhya becomes her unconscious cognition where one finds only disgust—the disgust of being proved a whore. After Raibhya is convinced that Yavakri has cornered Vishakha to dishonour his family, Raibhya's anger—the emotion of *krodh* overpowers him and his *Krodh* bursts like volcano:

> Raibhya: You whore—you roving whore! I could reduce you to ashes—turn you into a fistful of dust—with a simple curse. But let that husband of yours handle you. Paravasu, Chief priest of the sacrifice! Let him clean up his own shit! Yavakri—so this is what ten years of austerities amount to! So be it. So Yavakri, now it's between you and me. Where's that pot of water? Bring it here. (20)

Raibhya invokes "Kritya" Bramha Rakshasa to challenge the sprititual powers of Yavakri. His passion represents *Roudra Rasa*. The creation of Bramha Rakshasa is symbolic of his *krodh*:

> Raibhya: Vishakha, go and tell your lover I accept his challenge. I shall invoke the 'kritya' and send a Brahma Rakshasa, a demon soul, after him. Let Yavakri save himself. He need only go and hide in his father's hermitage. I loved my brother and will not desecrate his altar. Let Yavakri cower in there like a dog. If he steps out, he will be dead. Tell him this, too—that if he can manage to stay alive for another twenty four hours, I Raibhya, shall accept defeat and enter fire. (20)

Emotion of disgust is felt. It is *Jugupsa*—the disgust of the head of the family expressed for daughter in law. His *Krodh* with its *sthayibhav*—anger produces *Roudra Rasa*. The rishi, the sage, the so-called learned priest of Vedas, acts like a demon because of his jealousy—a jealousy that emanates from the physical passion of human mind. Vishakha at once tries to manage herself and overcomes the fear, which was deserting her a moment earlier. She no doubt, has a strong liking for Yavakri. She in her meeting with Yavakri concedes to her unwilling marriage with Paravasu. She, like a true lover, is ready to bear the consequences. She urges Raibhya:

> Vishakha: No, please. Don't do anything to him. It's my fault. Please don't harm Yavakri. I'm willing to face the consequences—punish me. Not him, please. (20)

*Vyabhicaribhavas* (universalized moods and feelings) are psychological in the sense that they are transformed through the sensory process. They are also helpful in intensifying the dominant emotions (*sthayi-bhavas*). Vishakha's dialogue with Aravasu is symbolic of her emotions of anxiety:

> Vishakha: (Wakes up) Aravasu, we must warn Yavakri. Instantly go to your uncle's hermitage.
>
> Aravasu: But Yavakri said he would be under the banyan tree near the black cliff.
>
> Vishakha: I'll run there. It's nearby. You go to the hermitage in case he's there Aravasu: But...but...
>
> Vishkha: Run, please I've never asked anything of you till now. Just this once. Go run. (20-21)

The last dialogue and the repetition of the work—run, go run—are symbolic of Vishakha's emotions of anxiety. Anxiety as subjective uneasiness of human mind brings into being some psychological disturbances. Vishakha rushes in search of Yavakri. Sometimes, the emotion of anxiety becomes a synonym to the emotion of fear. Psychology affirms that in the emotional condition of anxiety, the individual is seen in a state of more or less suspicion and worry. Psychological symptoms such as tension, irritation and shivering can be observed at such time. In the background of this anxiety, psychological feeling of weakness and insecurity function. In a state of anxiety all the physical powers of the individual are concentrated, as a result of which he gains the ability to face the situation or to prepare to escape from it. Sigmund Freud also supports some positive personality traits of anxiety:

> The major dynamic function of anxiety... operates at the unconscious level in the form of a warning signal to the ego of impending danger from inner impulses. Development of this function accompanies the gradual acquisition of judgement capacity by the ego... ability to judge and anticipate a threat results in the taming of anxiety through the creation of manipulatable replicas of potential traumas.[9]

Thus latent emotion of *bhaya*—fear—is worked out. The *sthayibhava* (permanent emotion) results into the realization of *rasa*. For arousing the latent emotion of aesthetic experience, Karnad has also worked out the theory of dream to display the unconscious mental forces. The metaphor of human psyche is symbolized through dream which universalizes the theory of emotions—the process of *sadharnikaran*. The theory of emotion of Indian aesthetics (*vibhavas, anubhavas*, and *sancharibhavas*) in showing the love of Nittilai and Aravasu is so skillfully worked out as it exhibits the universal validity of human emotions. The dialogue between Arvasu and Nittilai brings out the heartbeat of young lovers to the surface:

> Arvasu: I couldn't sleep a wink last night. Woke up in a cold sweat every time. I thought of your elders...........
>
> Nittilai: You are a fusspot. You've known them for years and after all, every young man about to get married goes through it. Just declare – Aravasu: Yes, I know, I know just stand there and say: " I want to take her as Nittilai: (shyly) Yes, more or less, that ! (5)

Arvasu grabs her hands and pulls her near but Nittilai tries to remind him that until a girl is married, she is not supposed to touch her husband to be. Arvasu as a true lover comments:

> I am about to jettison my caste, my people, my whole past for you. Can't you forget a minor custom for my sake? Nittilai: It's a nice custom, sensible, Worth observing. (6)

Aravasu gives up his Brahmanical order of life for wetting with the rains of Nittilai's life. He becomes "a low caste actor" (41) He peeps into the conspiracy of his elder brother and father and shares it with Nittilai and selects a profession of acting for her sake. Arvasu undergoes inner conflict which is the soul of drama. The nightmares of Arvasu are known as Puravavasna.

> Nittilai: You've always wanted to act. As long as remember. What will you do otherwise? Brood over Paravasu ? Whip yourself into a frenzy of anxiety over Me?
>
> Aravasu: I' am afraid.
>
> Nittialai: What's there to fear?
>
> Aravasu: It's the nightmare I told you about. I am dying of thirst. But there's no water. Then I peep into a huge well. There's water there, but it has my reflection in. I stare at it. And the reflection snarls: 'Why are you staring, wretch? Go away.' It says: 'You think so, do you, you swollen headed doll of flesh? I'll show you.' And the reflection leaps out of the water. Gouges my eyes out. Chews up my face in its jaws. I scream, but I have no face........It keeps on returning, that nightmare, so that now I'm not at all sure it's me standing here and not my reflection, all ready to attack.
>
> Nittilai: How long are you going to turn your face away from it then? Face it. (He looks at her in surprise.)

Not in hate, Aravasu. In the play. Show him how good you are. I'm sure the play will wash off the fear—the anger (He nods). (51)

The dream content exhibits the universal validity of human emotions:

> The form of thought which has been studied most intensively from the stand point of unconscious mental processes is, of course, the dream........ A fair amount of dream content stems from events of the day (day residues) thoughts prior to falling asleep, or even sounds heard while sleeping, simple, associating links one idea to the next.[10]

The dialogue between Aravasu and Nittilai is symbolic of their respective inner conflict. The contextual referents of the word determine its denotative and suggestive meanings apart from its connotative meaning. To a responsive reader, the perception of the guilt of Paravasu takes place ever before it is being translated into language:

Nittilai: I almost died when I heard they'd thrashed you. I got up and.......ran all the way here.

Aravasu: I went back to meet Paravasu.

(Excited)

That night I had to know why. What had I done? I thought he might tell me if I went to him secretly. So I went back at night. But he never came out.

Nittiali........I like you. (4)

*The Fire and The Rain* displays complicated human relationships symbolically. It abounds in its hard waves texture of the riches of psychology. It depicts the jealousy of man against man, father against son, brother against brother, wife against husband, high caste against low caste human beings. Jealousy crosses the boundary of this earth, sometimes the heart and brain. In this play we discover man against God, freedom against bondage, rituals against sacrifices, hate against love, attraction against repulsion, illusion against reality, passion against the fact, knowledge against the ignorance, falsehood against truth, arrogance against generosity, and *vijay* against *parajaya*. Girish Karnad focuses the contrastive elements in the notes appended to the end of the play:

> Thus the phrases *Agni Mattu Male*, in addition to counter pointing seem as antagonistic, also sets up several oppositions: between an Indo-Aryan (Sanskrit) and Dravidan (Kannad) language, between the pan-indic and the regional points of view, between the elevated and the mundane, even perhaps between...sacred and secular (here one needs to tread cautiously). (63)

In the development of these opposite elements, many kinds of *rasas* are experienced by the responsive reader—*Sringar Rasa, Bibhatsa Rasa, Veer Rasa, Raudra Rasa. Rasa* is the final goal of any art expression according to Indian aesthetics *The Fire and The Rain* is a dynamic combination of various art forms – music, dance, party etc.—the finest vehicle of all *rasas*. Dr. G. Vijaya Vardhana also supports the dominance of a single *rasa* in any poetic or dramatic composition:

> In a poem or a drama, one dominant *rasa* must prevail throughout, and the other subsidiary *rasas* should help its intensification. The poet constructs his plot in accordance with the *rasas* to be presented. He leaves out incidents of the original story, introduces new situations so that the *rasa* he intends conveying is best realized...the motif behind *prakarna* and *prabandha* – *Vakrata* is the proper manifestation of *rasas*.[11]

The development of the structure plan of *The Fire and The Rain* can be obsderved symbolically into three parallel streams: Raibhya and Vishakha at the hermitage, the sacrificial place with Paravasu as the Cheif Priest and the love story of Nittilai and Aravasu as the actors in a theatrical performance. Some Western influences on Karnad can be traced in the development of theatrical art in this play. The structural link with the original myth of *Mahabharat* displays Indian ethos and modern apathy towards complicated human relationships. The healthy relationship between Nittilai and Aravasu envelopes our heart since beginning. Nittilai's recalling back the words of her father for showing the hypocrisy of these high caste people – "The high caste men are glad enough to bed our women but not to wed them" (8) inspires Aravasu to the extent that he gives up Bramhanical order of life for the love of Nittialai who has been shown as a low caste human being. Acting is prohibited for the high caste. But Aravasu is happy to become 'a low caste actor'. *The Queen in Bali*: The Sacrifice accepts the low caste ugly looking mahout leaving the king and breaking the barriers of relationships between husband and wife, mother-in-law and daughter-in-law. Nirgunia—a married woman in *Nachhyo Bahuta Gopal* breaks off all the shackles of high caste family and marries willingly an untouchable protesting against the injustice of society. Ammu in *The God of Small Things* casts off morality of divorcehood and gives her body in her dreams to an untouchable Velutha. A lover who rejects his caste, ignores his prestige can confront even God to win his love. But there is something more precious in his heart, something which binds him to leave his love for higher achievements and it is Karuna, it is sacrifice, it is the thing which gives a seat of high appreciation to a man, who is adorned and worshiped like God – Karuna ke Sagar. The theory of *rasa* cannot be completed ignoring *karun rasa* because the modern age is the age of *karuna, bhavanaka* and *vibhatsa*. The dialogue between Indra and Aravasu has raised this mood to a pitch where the pathos of human existence is felt in terms of loss of virtue—the most loving object at least for a lover. One of Bhavbhuti's character declared Karuna to be *rasa* of *rasas*:

> Eka rasah Karuna evanimittabhedad
> Bhinnah prathak prathag ivasravate vibratian
> Avarta budbudatarangamayan vikaran
> Ambhavatha sahtmeva tu tal samagram.[12]

*Karuna* emerges from the destruction of the desirable and approach of the undesirable: 'I stanasadanistapteh karunakhyo rasabhavet'. Commenting on the verse, Madan Mohan Jha has explained that it is not necessary that the *Ista* (the desirable) must be a human being, it may be a being other than man or animate object. In the present context it is Aravasu who is aware of the mystery of life and death, it is he who swings between his two-halves, the egoistic and altruistic impulses of human mind. Aravasu—a passion ridden man—begging from Indra the life of Nittilai back – changes the content of his boon and begs now from Indra the release of Bramha Rakshasa. Aravasu's heart throbs with Karuna for Bramha Rakshasa who also stamps the superior validity of man for performing the deeds of mercy and compassion:

> I don't forgive. I can't. But you are human being. You are capable of mercy. You can understand pain and sufferings as the gods can't. (61)

The world of God with the concept of immortality is ridiculed and cyclic phenomena of death pertaining to human life is approved for its dynamic approach. The *Sringara* of love is essentially spiritual as conceived by Indians and in Indian cultural ethos. The Indian concept of love is never to possess and is always to efface oneself and to forget oneself. That is why it is raised to the rank of a vehicle which can freely reach God.

## NOTES

1. Girish Karnad. 1998. *The Fire and The Rain*. New Delhi: Oxford University Press. Preface. All subsequent references are to this addition and page number follows each citation.
2. Laxmi Chandrashekhar. 1999. *Plays, Players, and Playwrights*. Delhi: B.R. Publishing Corporation. 96-97.
3. Madhusudan Shastri (ed), *Natyashastram*. 677.
4. *Dhvnyaloka*. 1.5
5. R.G. Joshi. 1984. *Myth in Indian Drama*. New Delhi: B.R. Publishing Corporation. 36.
6. Madhusudan Shastri (ed), *Natyasastram*. 689.
7. R.L. Singhal. 1977. *Aristotle and Bharata: A Comparative Study of their Theories of Drama*. Hoshiarpur: Sadhu Ashram. 32.
8. Sigmund Freud. *The Ego and the Id* (Trans). Hogarth: London.
9. ——. 1938. *The Problem of Anxiety*, Newyork Nartan Press.
10. Gerald S. Blum. 1969. *Psychodynamics: The Science of Unconscious Mental Forces*, New Delhi: Prentice Hall.
11. Vijaya Vardhana. 1970. *Qualities of Sanskrit Poetics*. Varanasi: Chowkhambha Sanskrit Series.
12. Bhavabhuti: *Uttarramcharitam*.

# A De Novo Vision on Theology and Monarchy in *Tughlaq*

10

*Sadhana Agrawal*

A Rhodes scholar at Oxford (1960-63) and a Bhabha fellow (1970-72), Girish Karnad (born on May 19, 1938) is "one of the foremost prolific writers"[1] in India writing in Kannada. He is, undoubtedly, "the most celebrated personalities among the living Indian dramatists today."[2] He is also a well-known T.V. artist, a film producer, and an actor. He has nine published plays to his credit to this date namely *Yayati, Tughlaq, Hayavadan, Anju Mallige, Naga-Mandala, The Fire and the Rain, Bali: The Sacrifice, Tale-Danda,* and *The Dreams of Tipu Sultan.* "His dramatic genius has employed the remote and forgotten particles (episodes) of Indian history, myths and folk-tales. ... But unlike his predecessors, Karnad's plays are not more costume plays or masks, but they are invested with contemporary relevance" (Bedre 36). His first play, *Yayati* (1961), "was a self-consciously existentialist drama on the theme of responsibility."[3] His second play, *Tughlaq* (1964),[4] "was an instant success on the stage. It was first produced in Karnad in 1965 and ... in 1970 there was an English production in Bombay which was a major success" (Murthy vii). His next play, *Hayavadan*, the best play of 1971, brought him the Natya Sangh award.

The present study is an humble attempt to examine the conflict between theology and monarchy in *Tughlaq* where Sultan Muhammad Tughlaq, the central figure of the play, stands for administrative reforms, for implementing the policy of Hindu-Muslim amity, recognition of merit, irrespective of caste and creed, reorganization of administrative machinery and taxation structure; establishment of an egalitarian society in which all shall enjoy justice, equality and fundamental human rights. The study also unravels how an idedalist and visionary Tughlaq radically deviates from the religious tenets in matter of politics and administration and how this departue from the holy tenets enrages the orthodox people and in what way they condemn, oppose and rebel against Tughlaq. The study finally rests on Karnad, the playwright, who has adroitly employed this conflict between theology and monarchy in his play, *Tughlaq* which, as L.K. Bhatnagar observes, "is the best play in the 'New Drama in India' series"[5], and which deals with a historical story and thus "focuses entirely the socio-psychological and politico-religious motifs of the Sultan-Muhammad Tughlaq" (Budholia 80). To ambitious and intriguing politicians religion has been a means to achieve political end. Tughlaq, the idealist visionary and scholarly Sultan belonging to the fourteenth century India, is torn between religion and politics. At the very outset of the play, the dramatist exposes the tension and precarious conditions of the country through the discourse of the subjects of Tughlaq and also unravels his practice of sacred rites, the science of religion and his statecraft and the science of government for fulfilling his highly selfish political motives. In politics idealism does not pay. It is bound to fail. That is why the ambitious Sultan Muhammad Tughlaq uses religion to achieve his ends and thus pollutes it in the world of politics. In *Tughlaq* persons like Ulema, Sayyids and Amirs also use religion as a political instrument.

*Tughlaq* is noted for its historical theme and contemporary relevance. It is relevant to modern India, which has been passing through a crucial stage due to the conflict between religion and monarchy. Karnad himself makes it clear in writing the play that he is "turning to traditions and history now and seeking an answer there"[6] for the failures of the present. Muhammad Tughlaq ascends the throne of Delhi to rule over his Kingdom impartially. He wants to give his "beloved people" peace, freedom, justic and progress. He says that his people would witness:

> ...how justice works in my kingdom—without any consideration of might or weakness, religion or creed. (3)

But his ascendancy over the throne of Delhi makes him "at once a dreamer and a man of action, benevolent and cruel, devout and godless. His two close associates—Barani, the scholarly historian and Najib, the politician seem to represent the two opposite selves of Tughlaq. Aziz, the wily time server appears to represent all those who took advantage of Sultan's visionary schemes and fooled him."[7] Ramamurthy is equally right when he says that Tughlaq is "at once an idealist and a crafty politician, an humanist and a tyrant, a man who has murdered sleep and yet not a Macbeth haunted by supernatural solicitations, a man who thinks and broods too much and yet not a Hamlet incapable of action or guilty or delay."[8] Indeed Tughlaq was at first an idealist but as time passed on, his idealism failed and he turned to be a shrewd politician, a callous and heartless murderer and intriguer who employed religion for his political motives and even hurled the country into turmoil and troubles. Thus the play "explores the paradox of pseudo-idealistic Sultan Muhammad Tughlaq, whose reign is regarded as a spectacular failure in India's history (Bhatnagar 88).

As soon as the play opens, it reveals the tensions and political upheavals of the country, "What's this country coming to!" (1). This very first sentence of Old Man introduces tension in the country. The old people who are staunch followers of Islam think that the country is not in safe hands. They fail to understand Tughlaq's idealism and reformatory zeal, and condemn him as an enemy of Islam. In fact, he is a devout Muslim with full faith in the *Holy Koran* but his rationalistic and ideal views are beyond the comprehension of his subjects. But the young people admire and support the liberal and secular policies of the Sultan, whose rationalistic and modernized attitude appeals to the youth. The Young Man says: "The country's in perfectly safe hand—safer than any you've seen before" (1). No other Sultan before Tughlaq allowed "a subject within a mile's distance" (1). It is he who made prayer five times a day compulsory for all Muslims as dictated in the *Koran*. As the Young Man says:

> Now you pray five times a day because that's the law and if you break it, you'll have the officers on your neck. Can you mention one earlier Sultan in whose time people read the Koran in the streets like now? (1)

The conflict between righteousness and statecraft, thus, begins in the very first scene of the play. Karnad has successfully used this confliect in *Tughlaq*. When Tughlaq ascended to the throne of India he found the circumstances not favourable to rule because the country was divided between Islam and Hinduism. There was much animosity between the Hindus and the Muslims. Tughlaq began to make efforts to bring about harmony between the two communities, justice and equality for all for the welfare of his people. Tughlaq said:

> May his moment burn bright and light up our path towards greater justice, equality, progress and peace—not just peace but a more purposeful life. (3)

The tensions deepened as soon as Tughlaq announced the policy to shift the capital. By temperament Tughlaq was a rationalist and a philosopher and he wanted to build up a powerful and united nation. The far-sighted Tughlaq realized that this could be achieved only when if his "beloved people" would extend their "support and cooperation" (3). He made himself clear by saying that "this is no mad whim of a tyrant. My ministers and I took this decision after careful thought and discussion" (3). The decision to shift the capital from Delhi to Daulatabad was taken because:

> My empire is large now and embraces the South and I need a capital which is its heart. Delhi is too near the border and as you well know its peace is never free from the fear of invaders. But for me the most important factor is that Daulatabad is a city of the Hindus and as the capital it will symbolize the bond between Muslims and Hindus which I wish to develop and strengthen in my Kingdom. I invite you all to accompany me to Daulatabad. This is only an invitation and not an order. Only those who have faith in me may come with me. With their help I shall build an empire which will be the envy of the world. (3-4).

Tughlaq's rash decision to change the capital from Delhi to Daulatabad is a turning point in *Tughlaq*, which results in untold and inexpressible suffering to the common people.

Religion, which aims at the fundamental unity of mankind was dragged into the dirty game of politics. The Sultan practiced the idea of brotherhood, which is very important in Islam, but it annoyed the ecclesiastics because it undermined their political interests. The efforts of the Sultan to bridge the difference between Hindus and Muslims invited anger and displeasure of the Mullahs and Maulavis. To unite them he, therefore, abolished the *jiziya* tax and openly declared that both Hindus and Muslims would be treated impartially and would be equal in the eyes of the law. But this made him a suspect both in the eyes of the Hindus and the Muslims. Thus his policy to unite them miserably failed.

Here it is to be noted that Hindus were treated as second-class citizens in their own country. By the power of the sword the Muslim conquered India and Islam was imposed even on unwilling Hindus. Hindus constantly lived in fear of their lives. Religious bigotry prevailed on a large scale. The Mullahs and Maulavis called the Hindus *Kafirs* or infidels. But the Sultan treated the Hindus as equal. He also tried to bridge the gulf between them. He believed in justice to all. The case of the Brahmin Vishun Prasad was considered just as the Kazi. He declared, "His Merciful Majesty is guilty of illegal appropriation of land" (2), and "The Kazi-Mumalik has further declared that in return for the land and in compensation of the privation resulting from its loss the said Vishnu Prasad should receive a grant of five hundred silver diners from the State Treasury...a post in the Civil Service to ensure him a regular and adequate income" (2-3). Nevertheless the Muslims wanted Muhammad to kick the infidels. As the Old Man says:

> Beware of the Hindu who embraces you. Before you know what, he'll turn Islam into another caste and call the Prophet an incarnation of his god. (2)

Even the court Guard insulted the Brahmin in whose favour the Kazi had decided the case. He tells:

> Perhaps You Highness will want an escort to see you safely home! Complaining against the Sultan! Bloody Infidel! Get going, I'm already late. (6)

Even Hindus who were prospering and were exempted from *jiziya* taxes never trusted on their counterparts. They bore with such insults silently. In *Tughlaq* a Hindu expresses his anguish in the following words:

> We didn't want an exemption! Look, when a Sultan kicks me in the teeth and says, "Pay up, you Hindu dog', I'm happy. I know I'm safe, But the moment a man comes along and says, 'I know you are a Hindu, but you are also a human being' – well, that makes me nervous. (2)

The young Muslim reacted sharply and violently to this statement of the Hindu and called him an "Ungrateful wretch."

The irony is that the cheats, ruffians, cut throats and murderers always exploit religious sentiments and the idealistic policies of the Government to suit their motives just as a Muslim *dhobi* who was a cheat, disguised himself as a Brahmin whose claim was considered just by the Kazi.

*Tughlaq* is relevant to modern India. When this play was written, Karnad was fully conscious of the parallelism between the reign of Tughlaq and the India of the Sixties. He was also aware of the prevailing frustration of the Nehru era. As U.R. Anantha Murthy says:

> ....it is a play of sixites, and reflects as no other play perhaps does the political mood of disillusionment which followed the Nehru era of idealism in the country. (vii-viii)

Karnad himself writes about the contemporaneity of Tughlaq (Enact, June 1971):

> What struck me absolutely about, Tughlaq's history was that it was contemporary. The fact that here was the most idealistic, the most intelligent king ever to come on the throne of Delhi.....and one of the greatest failures also. And within a span of twenty years this tremendously capable man had gone to pieces. This seemed to be both due to his idealism as well as the shortcomings within him, such as his

> impatience, his cruelty, his feeling that he had the only correct answer. And I felt in the early sixties India had also come very far in the same direction the twenty-year period seemed to me very much a striking parallel. (viii)

The "striking parallel" presents a contrast between the political instability during the reign of Tughlaq and the social nostalgia of Delhi in the sixties.

In his introduction to the play, U.R. Anantha Murthy writes that Karnad makes the leitmotiv of the play prayer, "in the scene where the Muslim chieftains along with Sheik Shams-ud-din, a pacifist priest, conspire to murder Tughlaq while at prayer. The use of prayer for murder is reminiscent of what Tughlaq himself did to kill his father. The prayer, which is most dear to Tughlaq, is vitiated by him as well as his enemies, is symbolic of the fact that his life is corrupted at its very source. The whole episode is ironic" (ix). The prayer is diseased at the source of the political ascendancy.

Politicians corrupt religion. Tughlaq, a staunch follower of Islam, misused religion and prayer for his political purposes like politicians. He killed his father and brother at prayer time in order to regain political power. No religious man would commit that sin. But Tughlaq and his enemies were not ashamed of corrupting prayer thereby giving a death blow to religion. Amirs, Sardars, Ratan Singh and Shihab-ud-din also hatched a conspiracy to kill Tughlaq at prayer time. Sheikh Shams-ud-din opposed that prayer should not be polluted by Sultan's murder. At this Shihab-ud-din sarcastically advocated:

> Does your Islam works only at prayer? You have persuaded me to do what I have sworn never to do – you, Your Holiness, I'm sure the Lord will not mind an interrupted prayer. (36)

However, Tughlaq comes to know about this conspiracy and he cunningly gets Shihab-ud-din's plan to murder him at prayer time failed. Ratan Singh who wanted to see the downfall of Shihab writes to the Sultan and so the Sultan is forewarned. When the Sulatn is praying, about twenty Hindu soldiers rush in with spears and surround the Amirs and drag out some of them. Muhammad's prayer goes on uninterrupted. After the prayer he talks Shihab who is more defiant than ever and asks, "Why did you go against me? What wrong have I done you?" (42).

> Get on with your killing, Muhammad.....Beware! You wan't be able to trap me with your wiles. I am not Ain-ul-Mulk to live crushed under your kindness.....You want to solve all problems in the flash of a dagger, don't you? But you can't stop this uprising now. (42)

Under a fit of frenzy, he stabs Shihab-ud-din and goes on stabbing him until Barani stops him saying, "Your Majesty, he's dead! Muhammad stops, then flings the dagger away in disgust" (43). After stabbing him he asks Barani in anguish, "Are all those I trust condemned to go down in history as traitors? What is happening? Tell me, Barani, will my reign be nothing more than a tortured scream which will stab the night and melt away in the silence?" (43). Tughlaq brings to mind the hopes he cherished:

> What hopes I had built up when I came to the throne! I had wanted every act in my kingdom to become a prayer, every prayer to become a further step in knowledge, every step to lead us nearer to God. But our prayers too are ridden with disease....(44)

Bhatnagar aptly points out: "Incidently, the exploitation of prayer for murder is a rehash of what Tughlaq himself did to liquidate his father. That prayer which holds so dear to his heart stands fouled by him as well as by his foes is symbolic of the fact that his life is tainted at its very source. The whole episode is marked by irony. Shihab-ud-din, an ideaslist, who has reposed great trust in Tughlaq's rule in the process, falls a prey to the crafty machinations of Ratan Singh who engineers the entire plot of murder for his own narrow selfish gains" (92-93).

Muhammad during discussion reminds his Step-Mother of the murder of Shihab-ud-din of Sampanshahr: "He was the first man I killed with my own hands. And I had a glimmer then of what now I know only too well" (66). After this murder he turns to be a shrewd politician. This creates abhorrence in Tughlaq for prayer, which was life and soul for him, and he passes an order for its exile from his Kingdom:

> There will be no more praying in the Kingdom, Najib. Anyone caught praying will be severely punished. Henceforth let the moment of prayer walk my streets in silence and leave without atrace. (44)

The word 'prayer' is repeated several times and it reverberates throughout the play. Karnad dexterously shows how prayer affects the ruler and the masses. Ambition for power and money vitiates prayer and religion. Prayer is used to achieve an end and is not an end in itself. The powerful, the prosperous can pray in peace. The poor who are exploited and are empty stomachs cannot even think of prayer. Their prayer is only to earn bread by the sweat of brow. To Tughlaq it was a masquerade to hide his guilty conscience and to the hungry people it was a luxury. In the atmosphere of atrocisousness, cruelty, killing, sobs and sighs, wailing and tears which India had during the reign of Muhammad, it was very difficult for the people to pray. Scene Eleven of the play reveals that crowds of citizens demand food, not prayer:

> First Man: Prayer! Prayer! Who wants prayers now?
>
> Second Man: Ask them to give us some food.
>
> First Man: There's no food. Food's only in the palace. It's prayer for us. (70)

And further,

> First Man: How long are we going to starve like this?
>
> Second Man: Just a fistful of rice—a piece of meat would be enough.
>
> First Man: We don't want any prayer. We want food.
>
> Several Voices: Yes, food—we want food—not prayer. (72)

The dramatist ironically presents Aziz, the *dhobi*, who had disguised himself as Brahmin. He now appears in the guise of the great grandson of His Imperial Holiness Abbasid, the Khalif of Baghdad. He is invited by the Sultan to Daulatabad to bless the country and to start the banned prayer. An announcement is made so that all the citizens may welcome His Holiness for,

This is a holy day for – us – a day of joy!

And its glory will be crowned by the fact that the Public Prayer, which has been mute in our land these five years, will be started again from next Friday. Henceforth every Muslim will pray five times a day as enjoined by the *Holy Koran* and declare himself a faithful slave of the Lord. (69).

Muhammad welcomes His Holiness with these words:

> We have waited for years for this joyful moment. Our streets have waited in silence for the moment when the call to the holy prayer will ring in them again. And each year has been a century. We have waited long, Your Holiness, and our sins have become shadows that entwine round our feet. They have become our dumbness and deprived us of prayer. They have become the fiery sun and burnt up our crops. Now the moment has come for me and my people to rejoice. Only you can save me now, Your Holiness, only the dust of your feet on my head can save me now. (71-72)

It is a great ironic act that Tughlaq, the mighty and the most powerful, falls at the feet of Ghiyas-ud-din Abbasid, disguised Aziz. The great and shrewd politician of his time wants to seek shelter at the feet of a religious man not knowing the dust of the feet he is taking on his head, is a very common man's dust. Here the great emperor becomes an object of pity and foolery as his dreams of the monarch are shattered. Politics fails and the realm of religion begins to prevail over politics. Karnad succeeds in showing in that the common man in disguise is more powerful than the Sultan for the royalty has to bow down to him. The last scene becomes more ironical because the Sultan, who initiates the prayer after five years, falls asleep.

The play *Tughlaq* is noted for its symbols. Four symbols like Prayer, sleep, the game of chess and the rose are used to heighten the effect of the play. As P. Bayapa Readdy remarks: "At the micro level, prayer symbolizes the religious idealism of Tughlaq. At the macro level, it connects man's unconscious need for divine protection and guidance in an hour of anguish. In the begining prayer is made compulsory but later it is banned for a few years and again it is revived. It is reduced to a mockery when the Sultan's life is threatened at the time of prayer. 'Sleep' on one level represents the need for rest in man's life. At the macro level it becomes symbolic of peace, which eludes man often. The rose is a symbol of the aesthetic and poetic sensibility of Tughlaq. It later on beomes a symbol of the withering away of all the dreams and ideals of Tughlaq. At the macro level, the game of chess is an ordinary game which is popular in India. It also symbolizes a political game in which an ordinary washerman checkmates the most intelligent and clever politician. Through this symbolist technique, the playwight has succeeded in creating the right political atmosphere..."[9]

Rulers and politicians use religion as a medium to befool the common man. They pollute religion by misusing it for fulfilling their dirty political motives. They are impious and corrupt both in religion and politics. Karnad unhesitatingly states that a shrewd and intriguing politician cannot hide his two faces and cannot make his double talk understood by the people at large. However loud the ruler may shout that he stands for the *Koran* and its tenets, he will have to face insurrection in the body politic as well as within himself. He will have to pay the penalty. The conflict of theology and monarchy is having sufficient strength even now. Those who try to mix religion with politics are bound to fail. They cannot rule along with religion. Religion cannot be used to serve the end of those who are in power becaue it preaches morals and expects morality from the people. It stands for virtue, goodness, righteousness and morel conduct. It is again politics as it thrives on intrigue, craftiness, dishonesty and deceit. The case of Tughlaq is no exception. What Karnad shows in *Tughlaq* is that the idealist and his idealism do not go hand in hand with a politician and his politics. The idealist is only a misnomer and he has to face challenges, which he tries to curb down in his own crafty manner. But the idealist Tughlaq fails in producing any lasting result. What he gains, as he tells, is: Not words but the sword—that's all I have to keep my faith in my mission" and "power, strength to shape my thoughts, strength to act, strength to recognize my self" (66). All his idealism is shattered in the game of politics and thrown to the winds. Even Barani who is the best of his advisors asks Muhammad:

> Your Majesty, there was a time when you believed in love, in peace, in God. What has happened to those ideals? You won't let your subject pray. You torture them for the smallest offence. Hang them on suspicion. Why this bloodshed? (56)

Religion is above petty considerations of caste, creed, class, faith whereas politics is a marsh of these objects. Religion can discipline the lawlessness of an autocrat or ruthless politician whereas politics can only spread a net of cheat to fulfill its corrupt motives. That's why Tughlaq uses religion as a mask to play his political moves and intrigues. Invitation of the Sheikh Imam-ud-din to Delhi is a plitical move to trap him. The Sheikh comes to address the people but gets disappointed to find no people at the meeting to hear him. The Sultan intends seeking directions from the Sheikh and making amends for the wrongs he has done to the country and Islam. It is a hoax to trap the Sheikh who finds Tughlaq guilty of "scores of transgressions" (20). The Sheikh vehemently says:

> But if one fails to understand what the *Koran* says one must ask the Sayyids and the Ulema. Instead you have put the best of them behind bars in the name of justice. (20)

The Sheikh opines that oplitics should be governed by religion. The secular Sultan opposes it and replies:

> They tried to indulge in politics—I couln't allow that. I have never denied the word of God, Sheikh Sahib, because it's my bread and drink. I need it most when the surrounding void pushes itself into my soul and starts putting out every light burning there. But I am alone in my life. My kingdom has millions—Muslims, Hindus, Jains.Yes, there is dirt and sickness in my kingdom. But why should I call on God to clean the dirt deposited by men? (20)

The above passage implies that the Sultan is not irreligious though secular. When the ecclesiastics do their best to oppose his liberal and secular policy, he uses religion as a trap to get rid of them. In the name of religion and in view of the safety of Muslims if war break out, the Sultan persuades Sheikh Imam-ud-din to go to Ainul-Mulk. With his message of peace for "He respects you as every Muslim in India does. He will trust your word... will you please go as my envoy and dissuade him from this folly?" (23) The Sheikh suspects his motives but Muhammad makes him sure by asking: "You can't deny that this war will mean a slaughter of Muslims at the hands of fellow-Muslims. Isn't that enough for the great Sheikh Imam-ud-din?" (23) At last the Sheikh accepts the offer and feels delighted to be the emissary of the Sultan. The Sultan's soldiers thus, treacherously kill him. The crafty intriguer and manipulator over-throw the fearless and tireless fighter for Islam. This incident proves that a politician can never behave in a religious manner and an ecclesiastic should not meddle with politics.

The murder of the Sheikh leads to the intrigues of the courtiers and other idealists of the kingdom. This happening unites the Hindus and the Muslims altogether to rise against the craftiness and tyranny of the Sultan. Shihab-ud-din, the most trusted of the friends of Sultan is persuaded to attend the meeting of the intriguers and at last to stand against the Sultan. Sheikh Shams-ud-din Tejuddarfim tells Shihab-ud-din that he is attending the meeting to save Islam not to "get mixed up in the treacherous games of politicians... But Allah isn't only for me, ... while tyranny crushes the faithful into dust, how can I continue to hide in my hole?" (32)

*Tughlaq* is of great interest as it combines religion and politics of an idealist and visionary Sultan Muhammad Tughlaq. It intends to show that idealism of the ruler will fail and will ruin the idealist. The concepts like secularism, equality and unity in a country like India are very much ahead of the times. In India people still are lead away by the saints and religious heads. They believe more their religious leaders than a politician. The fiery speeches of the religious saint swing people this side or that side for the vote. People still are befooled by them as they were during the reign of Tughlaq. Thus the life of the people is governed and corrupted by the interaction of the saints and the politicians.

Tughlaq, who pretends to be a true follower of religion, commits numberless murders to retain his monarchy. He commits patricide, fratricide and wipes off the religious and political leaders like Imam-ud-din and Shihab-ud-din for his kingship. He tells the cause of murdering them to his Step-Mother in a simple way. "They couldn't bear the weight of their crown. They couldn't leave it aside so they died senile in their youth or were murdered" (11). When Step-Mother accepts that she has murdered Najib, Muhammad denies to accept this truth. But when she argues, "It was easier than killing one's father or brother. It was better than killing Sheikh Imam-ud-din," Muhammad replies, "I killed them for an ideal. Don't know its results? Don't you think I've suffered from the curse? My mother won't speak to me—I can't ever look into a mirror for fear of seeing their faces in it" (65). Muhammad is torn in finding peace in his own kingdom that "has become a kitchen of death" (65). There is only one punishment for treachery, he tells his Step-Mother, it is death. And for killing Najab he orders even his Step-Mother whom he loves more than anyone else to be stoned, dragged and killed. But these murders don't bring him peace. They tear him from within. He feels lonely and frustrated. In such torn and wretched state he seeks the shelter of God who alone can save him from misery and the ghosts of the murdered. Only He can help him to be a man. For this all of a sudden Tughlaq, the mighty murderer, plunderer and sinner, falls to his knees and clutches his hands to his breast to pray:

> God, God in Heaven, please help me. Please don't let go of my hand. My skin drops with blood and I don't know how much of it is mine and how much of others. I started in Your path, Lord, why am I wandering naked in this desert now ? I started in search of you. Why am I become a pig rolling in this gory mud? Raise me. Clean me. Cover me with your Infinite Mercy. I can only clutch at the hem of Your Cloak with my bloody fingers and plead. I can only

beg—have pity on me. I have no one but You now. Only You... You... You... You..." (67)

The above passage reveals a Faustian cry of anguish, which comes from the mouth of a Sultan. This Sultan uses his opponents like pawns on the chessboard of politics and unscrupulously kills them. Tughlaq even fails to offer prayer, which is reintroduced after an interval of five years when Ghiyas-ud-din Abbasid disguished Aziz comes to Daulatabad to bless him. He falls soundly asleep and gets up when the Muezzin's call to prayer fades away.

In *Tughlaq*, Girish Karnad presents a *de novo* vision on religion and politics, religious saints cannot wash away filth from society. "When it comes to washing away filth no saint is a match for a *dhobi*" (82), tells Aziz, the *dhobi*, masquerading as a saint, when ironically exposed, he pleads with the Sultan for his life. True religious spirit but not the orthodox religion of priests can discipline lawless and unscrupulous autocrats and politicians who unwittingly hurl their country and countrymen into the maelstrom of penury, starvation, murder and bloodshed. It has been proved that mixing of religion and politics always results in national disaster. Muhammad Tughlaq, a celebrated scholar and idealist, failed because, as Sheikh Imam-ud-din said, he mixed religion with his politics. The basic need of the people is food, not prayer, hence the word 'prayer' has lost its relevance in the play. Religion is not a political weapon and so it should not be misused.

It is worthwhile to sum up our discussion with these words: "It is high time that a serious thought is given to prescribing models of Indian writing in English of the kind of Tughlaq for our students studying at different levels and places. Equally rewarding can be exercise of disseminating them abroad!" (Bhatnagar 94).

## NOTES

1. O.P. Budholia, 1999-2000. 'The Dramatic Art of Girish Karnad', ed. A.N. Dwivedi, *Studies in Contemporary Indian English Drama*, Ludhiana: Kalyani Publishers, 80.

2. R.T. Bedre, Dec 2005. 'The Portrait of a Visionary: Karnad's *The Dreams of Tipu Sultan*', *The Quest,* Vol. 19. No. 236.
3. U.R. Anantha Murthy, 1975. *'Introduction to Tughlaq'*, Girish Karnad's *Tughlaq*. New Delhi: Oxford University Press: vii.
4. All the page references are to Girish Karnad, *Tughlaq* 1975. New Delhi: Oxford University Press. First published 1975. Twenty fourth impression 2003.
5. L.K. Bhatnagar, 1999-2000. 'Karnad's Tughlaq: A Critique', ed. A.N. Dwivedi, *Studies in Contemporary Indian English Drama*, Ludhiana: Kalyani Publishers, 88.
6. Girish Karnad, 1994. *Three Plays—Naga Mandala, Hayavadan, and Tughlaq*, New Delhi: Oxford University Press, 191.
7. M.K. Naik, 1982. *A History of Indian English Literature*, New Delhi: Sahitya Akademi, 262.
8. K.S. Ramamurthy. 1990 'He That Playeth the Sultan: *A Study of Tughlaq*', ed. Sudhakar Pandey and Freya Taraporewala, *Studies in Contemporary Indian Drama*, New Delhi: Prestige, 42.
9. P. Bayapa Reddy. 1990. *The Theatrical Representation of History, Studies in Indian Writing: With a Focus on Indian English Drama*, New Delhi: Prestige, 51.

# Symbolism in Girish Karnad's Play – *Tughlaq*

11

*Kranti Mishra*

Girish Karnad is one of the greatest Indian dramatists writing in English. He is a pioneer in the field of new drama and all his plays are actable. Karnad is a versatile genius. He is a film producer, an actor and a T.V. artist and also a playwright all in one.

This man of versatile genius, now fifty-three years old, was born at Matheson near Bombay is 1938. He had been a Rhodes scholar at Oxford from 1960 to 1963 and a Bhabha fellow from 1970 to 1972. He was also a visiting professor and a resident scholar at the Chicago University for some time. Girish Karnad wanted to be a poet but circumstances made him an dramatist. He himself tells us, "I wanted to be a poet, the greatest ambition in my life. At the age of 22, I realized I would not be a poet, but only a Play Wright."

He is one of the outstanding dramatists in modern Indian English drama. His work has the tone and expression of great drama. He has the genius and the power to transfer any situation into aesthete experience. Karnad imparted real dramatic verse to the technique of Indian English drama. This is his abiding contribution.

He has five or six plays to his credit, the best of them being *Yayati, Tughlaq* and *Hayavadana*. He himself translated the first two plays into English, while the last one has been translated only into Hindi. Myth, history and folk tales form the basics of these plays.

Karnad was deeply influenced by the naturalistic drama of Isben, Shaw and Shakespeare, the Natak Company plays of his home time which he frequently enjoyed in the company of his parents also influenced him.

As a dramatist, Girish Karnad is an existentialist. Existentialism implies consciousness of the self in the world of lived experience. It also implies problems of self-hood, search of identity, isolation and frustration. Karnad's style is simple, straightforward and idiomatic. Girish Karnad, who has been a Rhodes scholar at Oxford, has great command over English. He chooses apt and appropriate words from a rich treasury of vocabulary. His words are suggestive and reveal both character and situation. He writes dialogues in lucid, pointed and precise language. His dialogue has decorum. It is crisp, precise pointed and full of dramatic verse. Karnad's characters use language, which suit their status and temperament.

Karnad employs the devices of dialogue, contrast, parallelism and irony for character delineation. Characterization and plot are correlated and only those points of character are emphasized which develop the plot. Karnad is an Indian writer in English and he has succeeded in creating a proper Indian Atmosphere. He has introduced a number of words from the Indian language into English. He has suitably Indianised his English.

His first play *Yayati* reinterprets an ancient myth from *Mahabharata* in modern context. It is an existentialist drama on the theme of responsibility.

*Hayavadana*, a bold and successful experiment is folk theme. Its plot comes from an ancient collection of stories in Sanskrit "Kathasaritsager". In *Hayavadana*, Karnad successfully uses the conventions and motifs of folk-tales and folk-theatre.

Karnad's second play is *Tughlaq* written in 1962. It was an immediate success and at once catapulted him to fame to the first rank of Indo-Anglian dramatists. Before writing *Tughluq*, Karnad delved deep into history. Tughluq was the most extra-ordinary character to come on the throne of Delhi in religion, in philosophy, in battle. *Tughlaq* is Girish Karnad's best play and his art and technique are best studied with reference to the play. It is a historical play and there is a judicious mixture of fact and fiction. Its plot is based on history. The central character Muhammad Tughlaq and a number of characters who surrounds him are historical but there are also characters like Aziz and Azam who are the dramatists' own invention. Both incident and situation are correlated with characters, events and incidents, which originate from the paradoxical actions of the protagonist. The plot is based on opposites and paradoxes intrigues brought under the discipline of art from its main basis.

*Tughlaq* has been set in the fourteenth century India and the dramatist has verily created the atmosphere of court intrigue, seditions, murderes and blood shed.

Symbols are essential words. They have great emotional and associated significance. They enlarge the expressive range of the language and make it more beautiful and forceful. Hence great writers always use symbols. Girish Karnad has also used number of symbols for these reasons in *Tughlaq*.

He uses chess, prayer and python as symbols in *Tughlaq*. The chess suggests the intrigue in Tughlaq's nature. As a skilled chess player he uses his political opponents as pawns on the chessboard of politics. Python suggests Tughlaq's barbarity and inhumanity. His spirit knows no respite or peace.

## THE CHESS SYMBOL

The chess has a very important significance in the play. The chess symbol shows how Tughlaq manipulates his political rivals and opponents as pawns on the chessboard of politics according to his sweet will.

As shown in the scene two Muhammad is bent over a chessboard smiling with suppressed excitement. Seeing his stepmother Tughlaq happily tells her, "I have just solved the most famous problem in chess. Even Al-Adli and Sarakhi said it was insoluble and it's so simple". He is thinking about the rebellion of Ain-ul-Mulk who is marching to Delhi. He has been the Sultan's childhood companion. Tughlaq who has not even six thousand soldiers, has solved the series problem of Ain-ul-mulk rebellions. A subtle political strategist Tughlaq while throwing pawns on the chessboard solves this complicated problem. Tughlaq knows that Sheikh-Imam-ud-din has been inciting rebellion against him in Kanpur. He invites the Sheikh to address a public meeting in Delhi to enlighten the citizen about his shortcomings. All arrangements have been made but nobody turns up to hear the Sheikh who resembles the Sultan. The Sheikh understands that it was a trap to befool him. Tughlaq humbly requests the Sheikh to go to Ain-ul-Mulk as a royal envoy and to dissuade him from his folly. The robes of honors for the royal envoy are brought The Sheikh puts them on. They stand facing each other. The dress makes them look even more alike. He goes to negotiate with Ain-ul-mulk. The Sheikh is killed. Ain-ul-mulk is surrendered and is pardoned.

## THE PRAYER SYMBOL

In Tughlaq symbol, which is used as theme, associated with a person or a thought is very significant. The Muslim chieftains along with Sheikh Shams-ud-din, a priest, conspire to murder Tughlaq at prayer time. The use of prayer to murder is reminiscent of what Tughlaq himself did to kill his father. Tughlaq is fanatic about prayer. The plan of murder fails due to his farsightedness and his secret knowledge of conspiracy. He realizes the futility of prayer and prohibits prayer in his kingdom. The word prayer has been used in an ironical way. In the play prayer is reintroduced after an interval of five years when Ghiyas-ud-din Abbasid comes to Daulatabad to bless the Sultan. The prayer symbol is the very basis of the play.

## AZIZ AND AAZAM AS SYMBOLS

Aziz and Aazam are cheaters who symbolize Opportunistic and unprincipled people who exploit the liberal ideas and welfare schemes of the democratic government to fulfill their own pockets. They feel pleasure when people die of hunger and starvation. To them politics is a profitable profession.

## PYTHON AS A SYMBOL

The python symbol shows Tughlaq's utter barbarity and in-humanity. The python also symbolizes the increased fierceness, brutality and bloodthirstiness of the Sultan. It is symbolic of the complete degeneration of his personality. From a human being, he has degenerated into a wild beast, a huge snake.

## DAULATABAD AS A SYMBOL

Daulatabad is a Hindu city. It is a symbol of Hindu-Muslim unity. So Muhammad transfers his capital from Delhi to Daulatabad. But the entire experiment is a failure. Instead of leading to prosperity and peace, it leads to bloodshed and utter chaos. This symbolism shows that even the best plans and ideas can be failed if people who work under it are as dishonest as Aziz and Aazam.

## SYMBOLIC USE OF BIRDS AND PREY

The vulture and other birds of prey who thrust then beaks into the flesh of Muhammad so that he knows no peace either by day or night, are also symbolic. They symbolize the frustration of an idealist and visionary, and his spiritual agony. Tughlaq who once was an idealist and visionary is now a frustrated person. All his visions and measures of reform have failed. His character has degenerated to such an extent that people have started calling him "Mad Tughlaq." That is the tragedy of idealism.

Thus Girish Karnad's *Tughlaq* is an immortal play, which shall be read and acted as long as English, is read and enjoyed. It is a great classic of Indo-English drama in which symbolism plays a very important role.

## REFERENCES

Girish Karnad's – *Tughlaq*.

M.K. Naik: *Critical Essays on Indian Writing in English*.

U.R. Anantha Murthy – *Critical Reviews on Karnad's Plays*.

# An Estimation of Vijay Tendulkar as a Playwright

12

*Smita Mishra*

Vijay Tendulkar, India's most turbulent and controversial dramatist, at the age of seventy-five, is still doing what he does best: writing with his uncompromising and merciless style about human frailties and hypocrisies that we live in our day to day life. Tendulkar has never craved for outdated or impossible subjects. Human existence, deep understanding of human psychology and expressing them through drama have been an obsession with him. He prefers restraint and simplicity to excessive freedom and gaudiness. The depiction of life in Tendulkar's plays has an invisible but solid foundation in his philosophy of life. The individual existence of man and his social existence, the harmony and disharmony between the two, form the essence of his thinking.

As Tendulkar has always vocalized different human relations and the tensions implied therein, so he plunged into violent currents and splashed irritatingly bold colours in *The Vultures*. The play is the story of a family consisting of abnormal members using and abusing each other for petty little greed, making life unbearable for the two innocent persons of tender sensitivities destined to live amongst them. *The Vultures* puts forth, through its characters, the distorted projections of the realities of common people, their agonies, frustrations, greed and avarice.

In the play Tendulkar portrays the ruthless violence that we witness in our socitey. It depicts violence in an upper middle class family. Competitiveness, individualism and their sequel lovelessness attacked the members and strained human relations within the family.[1] When material things become more important than human relations, loveless people resort to any gross atrocity. As Tendulkar feels, violence becomes a natural consequence of such a situation. The play throws light on the impairment of human relations even within the family caused by lovelessness. It elucidates how lovelessness can bring about most inhuman violence even within a family.[2]

Tendulkar's *Sakharam Binder* created dramatic history by challenging the Censor Board because it was initially banned. Tendulkar's depiction of a character who rejects the artificial values imposed by the society and the use of extremely vulgar and outspoken language incensed the Censor authorities. Later the restrictions were lifted and the play became extremely popular.[3] Sakharam is frank and outspoken and he tries to work out an independent philosophy of life, with no sense of false obligations.[4] He has no social taboos. He drinks heavily, has no sense of guilt and admits to all his vices. Sakharam is a bitter critic of the institution of marriage and attacks husbands while pitying wives. He assures every women he brings home of his 'good' treatment. He frames certain rules for his women companions. Later, he tells Champa, one who enters after Laxmi's exit, that a woman's job is to make the food herself. Thus, Sakharam, in his passionate rejection of the traditional and moral values, tends to contradict himself in word and deed in the absence of well-considered moral alternatives.

Though Sakharam keeps on repeating time and again in the play that he is no husband to forget common decency, he wants that the woman who, lives with him shall have to be a wife to him. So, while he poses to be a saviour, he presents the picture of a brutal perpetrator and wretched victim of all that is bad in society regarding the man-woman relationship.[5]

*Kanyadaan*, the most controversial of all the plays, dwells on an extremely sensitive social and political issue, namely, the conflict between the upper castes and *Dalits*, a phenomenon still rampantly prevalent in several parts of India. Despite fifty five years of independence *Dalits* continue to suffer abject misery and ill-treatment at the hands of the upper castes. Politicians, instead of trying to uproot this evil, seem to capitalize on it.

An over-idealistic democratic couple, their revolutionary daughter who marries a down caste poet and gets disillusioned in the consequent turn of events due to the unexpectedly barbaric behaviour of her life partner are presented on stage by Tendulkar with a contemporary relevance. These extraordinary and selectively unique characters represent the plight and realities of common people, their aspirations, sufferings, frustrations and agonies. The play concerns the unmistakable ambivalence inherent in the words and deeds of both the promoters and the beneficiaries of *Dalit* upliftment programmes. The play also exposes the oppression, exploitation and humiliation of women by their father and husband. It is an example of a situation where, in a partiarchal society, a woman is used or downtrodden by man to suit his purposes. Though the book received 'Saraswati Samman', it provoked *chappal* throwing when the play was staged in Marathi. Tendulkar syas: "as its creator I respect both verdicts."

In *Silence! The Court is in Session* Tendulkar has raised several questions on love, sex, violence, marriage and moral values prevalent in the society. In this play he has highlighted certain important themes. The men who have accused Benare are themselves the frustrated flops of the society who are lashing out their failure in an assault on a young woman.[6] All the male characters in the play are superficial, unkind and cruel. A young woman belonging to the middle class in our country is denied the privilege of living a decent life, of becoming a mother. The so-called intellectual Professor Damle after using her does not come forward to protect her. An extreme form of powerlessness for a woman is the denial to bear a child. This kind of sheer cruelty and inhumanity is inherent in all these characters because they know no way of relating to other people except by exploitation.

Tendulkar depicts Benare as a modern woman who is capable of protecting herself, and her body in a male dominated society. He does not let Benare kill herself or feel shy of the whole episode, but makes her fight till the end. She knows that the male who is responsible for her fate will not confess; yet she is determined to defend herself. The intellectual who is responsible for Benare's humiliating condition goes unscathed and unnoticed, but she is deposed literally naked in front of these men. The very men who give lectures on the dignity of woman and motherhood are responsible for inflicting shame and indignity on her.

The image of a woman in contemporary Indian literature has changed drastically. No more a woman is considered or portrayed as weak, or falling at the feet of her husband or trying to please him always. Generally in Indian society a good woman is synonymous with a doormat type wife. But modern writers have tried to transform this image of woman by portraying them in a more realistic manner. One such writer is Vijay Tendulkar, and his play *Kamala* brings forth woman in a different role.

*Kamala* by Tendulkar, questions the false social norms prevalent in the society which asks everyone to conform to its yardstick of decorum and propriety. It says that irregular and abnormal behaviour is not to be tolerated. No reasons are good enough to justify and find excuses for a person's erratic behaviour. The play explored the layers of the internal mind and exposes the psychological findings. An unfortunate woman sold away in the flesh market and a so-called happy housewife married to a daring journalist, and both have a revelation of finding themselves on a common platform of sexual slavery in this male dominated world moved Tendulkar to probe into their pathetic condition.

*Safar*, a hard hitting play by Tendulkar deftly unveils the complex and mulish attitudes that permeate our middle-class society.[7] They are the hideously ugly attitudes that are likely to make men topple down. The central character is locked within the confines of home by his over-protective parents. At one end while he is content with the arrangements, he wants to break away. But fear, anger, hatred, loath impede his need to go ahead in his journey of life. Finally, what remains is a doleful, frustrated individual (symbolic of our society), resigned to his pitiable fate. The play is a fine protrayal of the complexities of human character.

Encounter in *Umbugland* expresses Tendulkar's impression about the politicians and their politics with poignant sarcasm. It reveals that the very life of politics is falsehood and hypocrisy and that the political language is a completely dishonest one. As in India, in the play also, "Democracy has become a synonym for autocracy or dictatorship."[8] as observed by E. Renuka. The play clarifies that one should not be true to oneself in politics. One has to become dehumanized. It is an exemplary piece of falsehood. Everyone in the play tells lies to one another so as to escape safely. It shows how the desire of rising higher and higher makes people suppress their humaneness. In their scramble for power they lose peace and happiness.

The play also exposes the role of government and the press in making people ignorant. It shows how leaders make their people mindless and how mindless people allow their leaders to be hypocritical. How the government arouses emotions in the people and paralyzes their faculty of thinking and rationality. In the story the Cabinet Ministers drive the mob against Vijaya, the queen who tactically turns against the Ministers themselves.

Tendulkar's highly controversial play *Ghasiram Kotwal* is based on the historical conflict between Nana Phadnavis and his henchman Ghasiram Kotwal. This ballet, a blend of spoken verse, varied music and highly original choreography, gave to the Marathi theatre an artistic experience worth cherishing for time immemorial. It relieved the folk roots of Marathi theatre in order to present a theme free from all its temporal and spatial bondages.

*Ghasiram Kotwal* tells the story of a person who, confronted with a world of hypocrisy and inhumanity, learns to play a careerist falling in line with prevailing ethics and becomes a martyr. Ghasiram's transformation from an ordinary person to the tyrannical executor of power and to an ordinary person again is more eventful than the story of Nana, a cult hero, as it is relevant in the modern context of individuals taking advantage of situations, using power and crashing in no time to impotence at the whims of more powerful players in the same game.

Nanas and Ghasirams will be there in every society as long as the hierarchy of power and alienation that is behind them continues to exist. The people of Pune think that Ghasiram is dead. But Ghasiram is dead only as a person while his role is very much alive and somebody will play the role again.[9] That's why Tendulkar himself aptly observes that he had in mind the emergence, the growth and the inevitable end of the Ghasirams; and also those who create and help Ghasirams to grow. The title of the play suggests the incident only and not the character, Ghasiram Kotwal. And because of the form incidentally Tendulkar de-glamorized the historical incident.

*Damn You Fate* poses to be just a fun, an amusement, a playful projection of fantasy, but proceeds to serious critical overtones either openly or suggestively. Here Tendulkar emerges as a sarcastic critic of the dirty game of politics. Two of his previous plays viz. *Ghasiram Kotwal* and *Encounter in Umbugland* did have distinct political thought and analysis. But they were satires, symbolic suggestions, parodies and oblique overtones, concealed under stage gimmicks, presentation-skills, music and such other things. Here it is a totally different case. In *Damn You Fate*, he has exploded his political thought on the stage for the first time. He has ridiculed the political personalities through a fantasy like presentation; but the real purpose behind it is to express the anger boiling in the mind of the common man. It is a warning signal to the selfish opportunist politicians.[10]

The drastically contrasting evaluations of a sacked CM either by common people or by the self satisfied crooked politician in the play poignantly unveils the vulgarity of the dirty politics and at the same time illuminates many reflections of so many contemporary politicians known to us. Treachery, deception, red-tapism, bureaucracy, showism, false promises, people's courts, television snobbery, suffocation of the Press, political dinners and tea parties, staged encounters with terrorists, deliberate killings of wrong people—everything finds its place in the spectrum of political strategies in this short play. T.V. covering of the public meetings of the Chief Ministers, slogans like 'strength the hands of the PM' and 'Mera Desh

Mahaan', references like purchasing the owner of the newspaper, uncover the masks over the familiar faces in contemporary politics and expose the sensitive nerves open. And all this comes in the manner of a very sharp parody.

In the works of Vijay Tendulkar the innovative use of form, whether it is the mock trial in *Silence! The Court is in Session*, or the human curtain in *Ghasiram Kotwal*, acts as a magical component in his plays. Tendulkar brought in novel forms in the form of drama, not just for the sake of experimentation but also to explore the fit and proper expressions to suit the especially demanding contents. He allowed the technique of film art to enter his plays with its apt use of 'darkness and light effect', 'freezing of the scenes', 'making the motion of the scene slow or fast', 'use of background music' etc. Tendulkar is the only writer who writes simple, natural, character-revealing dialogues that can reach poetic heights when required.

The style of Tendulkar in his plays is biting and demotic modelled on the language, rhythms and association of ordinary speech. He has changed the form and pattern of the Indian drama by developing the flexible as well as carefully crafted forms, modes of recitation and story telling specific to his region. He has managed to bridge the gulf between the traditional and modern theatre by creating a new vibrant theatrical form, an example of which is *Ghasiram Kotwal*, the folk drama format, with its elaborate use of facial expressions, mime, song, dance and symbolic use of stage techniques which contribute to the universal appeal of the play. In the play a human curtain is formed and dispersed for dramatic purposes from time to time according to the requirements. The Marathi tradition of 'tamasha' and 'sutradhar' has also been used in the play that interposes in the proceedings to keep the audience abreast of things.

In *Silence! The Court is in Session* the mock trail makes a deft stroke on the part of Tendulkar's dramatic genius functioning almost like a 'play within a play'. Benare who has all along been baiting her male counterparts, ends up being ruthlessly hunted and baited by them all. The mock trail also helps the playwright to expose to his audience the cruelty latent in the collective psyche of the city-bred male chauvinists of the metropolis.

Similarly in *Kamala* there are significant spells of silence, registering the sensitive trajectories of thought processes in the minds of the characters. In the play the motif of the hectic phone calls contribute to the principal theme of the play. In *Encounter in Umbugland* the two masked actors with large pens, arrive at regular intervals to make observations on the recent development Rajaninath's self-compassionate songs revealing the past happenings in the Pitale family in *The Vultures* is totally innovative and outstanding. Again *Safar* and *Damn You Fate* stand next in the line of Tendulkar's plays that leave the audience/reader speechless with admiration.

Tendulkar's plays are experiments of an intense and depper impulse and not just a matter of superficial innovations. He has experimented with almost all aspects of drama—content, acting, stage direction and audience communication. Hence, his play are structurally, free from any recognizable flaws. Never for a moment does he indulge in anything for the sake of theatricality. The plots always evolve and unfold themselves rather imperceptibly. Every time the audience have the satisfaction of witnessing a few rare moments of pure aesthetic delight and intellectual insight designed by an extremely powerful artist.

Tendulkar's plays helped to refind Marathi drama that was so far polluted by propaganda for political awakening, and social reforms, cheap and vulgar entertainment. The reason being that he started writing his plays after delving deep into human relations. He never indulged in painting superficial conflicts in gaudy colours, rather he painted human relationship in today's socio-politic surroundings effectively in pastel shades.

## NOTES

1. M.S. Babu. 1990. "Spiritual Deformity" in *India Drama Today*, Delhi: Prestige Books. 139.
2. "Spiritual Deformity". 143.
3. Geeta Kumar, "Portrayal of Women in Tendulkar's Sakharam Binder and Shantata! Court Chalu Ahe" in *New Directions in Indian Drama* (eds.) S. Pandey and Freya Barwa. Delhi: Prestige Books. 24.

4. Ashok H. Desai, "Censorship and Sakharam Binder", Preface to Sakharam Binder. 7.
5. E. Renuka, "Casanova as the Saviour: A Study of Vijay Tendulkar's Sakharam Binder" in *New Directions in Indian Drama.* 34.
6. Veena Noble Dass, "Women Characters in the Plays of Vijay Tendulkar" in *New Directions in Indian Drama.* 10.
7. Ajay C. Joshi, "Cycle of Life", *The Indian Express* Front Page, Satudray, February 27, 1999 (available on the website *www.expressindia.com*).
8. E. Renuka. 1984. "All about Umbugland: A Study of Vijay Tendulkar's Play", Diss. Kakatiya University. 147.
9. M.S. Babu. 1990. "Political Deformity" in *Indian Drama Today*, Delhi: Prestige Books. p. 77.
10. "Two Recent Plays of Vijay Tendulkar". 48.

# Mechanism of Girish Karnad as a Dramatist

13

*Roopesh Chaturvedi and Rohini Dubey*

Seemingly following the Aristotelian dictum that the plot of a drama cannot be invented and a playwright should pick up already existing one, Girish Karnad seldom tends of opt for the fabrication of his own never-ever-before-kind of plots. Like numerous dramatists from the past, he prefers to be a narrator of an old tale from strikingly new angle extending abundance of uneasiness to the amazed viewers. Karnad is not mind boggling, never thought provoking but he is always the giver of emotional and intellectual discomfort to the viewers. By unearthing folklore not extensively known outside its place of origin, he popularizes cult, culture and queerness associated with Indian history and mythology. A part from the language used, the theory of existentialism is another westernized aspect of the literary contribution of Girish Raghunath Karnad.

The literary works have always been in existence and the necessity of their existence has always been questioned but in this part the role and need of a critic come in the scene. Comedy is the crooked representation of life. Many critics censor it for this reason. Tragedy is purposeful and dignified purgates. Therefore should be written and staged upon. Willing suspension of disbelief explains the existence and association of a viewer with a piece of literary production. In case of Karnad any fix notion explaining the mechanism of his writing cannot be easily located. For he does not seem to write complete comedy or full tragic plays. Thereby he is not trying to make his position as a classist as per the recommendation of Aristotle. Karnad displays his own dignity in his writing where a viewer does not anticipate a comic situation with the purpose of comic relief or utter tragedy without rags of hope. Karnad is not a writer of comic plays or comic scene but he is humorous. He is not utterly tragic with no hope left. He is tragic with some silver lining in dark clouds. Karnad maintains his even description of happenings with an element of little surprise. But above all his extension of uneasiness to the viewer and direct significance of his plays to the modern context enable him to be a successful playwright.

Karnad is, in a true sense, a recreational writer with reinforced ranges of stories retold. *Yayati* is the first contribution from his pen. The play is an elaboration of an ancient myth from Indian epic *Mahabharat*. The plot is mythical but the content is modern. The story revolves around the character of Yayati—a king who in the prime of his life is cursed to old age and he goes around asking people "Will you take my old age? Will you take my old age?" No one accepts, except his own son Puru. Ultimately the son becomes old and the father becomes young. The presentation of the myth, no doubt, irritates the sensibilities of the orthodox viewers but the more enlightened critics may appreciate the new approach of the play. What impresses the modern spectators of the play is the reinterpretation of the ancient myth is the light of the contemporary world. The present context can be seen in the play as each and every spectator finds his own case being staged upon. One's parents demanding that their son should behave in a particular way, even though the future of the son seems to be opening up in another way. This is how in the play the myth in some ways gives exact expression to the numerous incidents taking place in various households. In *Yayati* the quest of the king and his son for the assertion of their being, despite limitations and failures, makes the play an excellent example of a composition based upon the then popular philosophy of existentialism.

Like *Yayati* Karnad pens *Tughlaq* in Kannad. Subsequently he translates it into English. In this play as well his typical mechanism of writing a play can easily be located. The play is based upon a plot that is taken from Indian history, i.e. not a novel plot. The play fits itself in the modern context in a way that due to the popular philosophy of existentialism to be considered mad was fashionable and was a matter of pride. Tughlaq seems to be fit in the frame of Madness. Tughlaq was the most extraordinary character to come on the throne. In every field he seems to have come before or after his time.

*Tughlaq*, at the same time can be described as an allegorical play reflecting the governance of the first prime minister of India, thereby, directly or indirectly hurting the sentiments of a big mass of fans with extending uneasiness by portraying Pt. Nehru in such a shabby light.

*Hayavadan*, the complete play about incompleteness, has been produced in typical Karnad's style that the plot taken from boldly experimented folk theme, which comes from *Kathasaritsagar*, an ancient collection of Sanskrit stories. Again the play is originally written in Kannad later on, translated in English. The dramatist successfully uses the conventions and motifs of folk theatre. Folk tales, masks, curtains, and dolls help in the creation of bizarre world sustaining uneasiness and the emotion of incompleteness among the viewers through the amazing display of haunting intellect without muscle power and *vice versa*. The search of identity in the midst of tangled relationship is the backbone of the play. Padmini rooted for the body of Kapila and the intellect of Devdatta is the sheer display of discomfort arising out of unquenchable desire to have two-in-one. Consequently two, Kapila and Devdatta kill themselves and Padmini transposes their heads. This act of Padmini reveals the ambiguous nature of human personality.

In *Nagmandal*, Karnad uses two oral tales (folk tales) from Karnataka related to him by Prof. A.K. Ramanujan. The element of discomfort for the viewers is highlighted by male chauvinism and by the display of human necessity to live in dreams by half truth. In modern ambience, men and women have to work in tandem to maintain their pace of progress. Women have displayed that they have drive to and enterprise as much as men have. The present generation shall be worse than blind Kurudava if it fails to give women their due place and respect in the society and worse than Kobra, if it fails to appreciate their potential. Rani and Naga's ultimate reconciling with the situation is edifying. It is no wisdom to remain stuck to the past, when future beckons the generation.

Apart from mentioned mechanisms, the ability of Karnad lies in the strength of universalizing the individuals and social predicaments. He meticulously uses folk tales, myths and legends giving them surprisingly modern dimensions in his plays. This is what makes him enjoy the exquisite reputation of being the most performed playwright abroad.

# Contributors

**Shubha Tiwari** is Head of the Dept. of English at A.P.S. University, Rewa, M.P.

**Dipika Sahai** is Reader at D.A.V. College, Kanpur, U.P.

**Ashok Kumar Sharma** is Reader at Feroze Gandhi College, Rae Bareli, U.P.

**Smita Mishra** has done her Ph.D. from C.S.M. Kanpur University, Kanpur.

**Jayadeep Sarangi** is Reader at Seva Bharati Mahavidyalaya, Midnapur, W.B.

**Ranjana Chanana** is Asst. Prof. at Govt. College, Chhatarpur, M.P.

**Sadhana Agrawal** is Asst. Prof. at Govt. College, Chhatarpur, M.P.

**Kranti Mishra** is a Contractual Lecturer at the Dept. of English, A.P.S. University, Rewa, M.P.

**Roopesh Chaturvedi** and **Rohini Dubey** are research scholars at A.P.S. University, Rewa, M.P.